"We owe a lot to Thomas Edison—if it wasn't for him, we'd be watching television by candlelight."
—Milton Berle

"Out, out, brief candle! Life's but a walking shadow, a poor player that struts and frets his hour upon the stage and then is heard no more: it is a tale told by an idiot, full of sound and fury, signifying nothing."
—William Shakespeare, Macbeth

"You know you're getting old when the candles cost more than the cake."
—Bob Hope

"Go within every day and find the inner strength so that the world will not blow your candle out."
—Katherine Dunham

"Curiosity is the wick in the candle of learning."
—William A. Ward

*"As a white candle
In a holy place,
So is the beauty
Of an aged face."*
—Joseph Campbell

*"I continue to create because writing is a labor
of love and also an act of defiance, a way to
light a candle in a gale wind."*
—Alice Childress

*"There are two ways of spreading light: To be
the candle or the mirror that reflects it."*
—Edith Wharton

*"We must view young people not as empty
bottles to be filled, but as candles to be lit."*
—Robert H. Shaffer

*"Life is no brief candle to me; it is a sort of
splendid torch which I've got a hold of for the
moment and I want to make it burn as brightly
as possible before handing it on to future
generations."*
—George Bernard Shaw (1856–1950)

"She would rather light a candle than curse the darkness, and her glow has warmed the world."
—Adlai Stevenson

"Make a candle to get light; read a book to get enlightened."
—Chinese proverb

My candle burns at both ends;
It will not last the night;
But ah, my foes, and oh, my friends—
It gives a lovely light.
—Edna St. Vincent Millay

"The best candle is understanding."
—Welsh Proverb

"A scholar is a candle which the love and desire of all men will light."
—Ralph Waldo Emerson

"To light one candle to God and another to the Devil is the principle of wisdom."
—José Bergamín

Mastering

Candle

Magick

Advanced Spells and
Charms for Every Rite

Patricia Telesco

New Page Books
A division of The Career Press, Inc.
Franklin Lakes, NJ

MASTERING CANDLE MAGICK

EDITED AND TYPESET BY KATE PRESTON

Cover design by Lu Rossman/Digi Dog Design

Printed in the U.S.A. by Book-mart Press

To order this title, please call toll-free 1-800-CAREER-1 (NJ and Canada: 201-848-0310) to order using VISA or MasterCard, or for further information on books from Career Press.

The Career Press, Inc., 3 Tice Road, PO Box 687,
Franklin Lakes, NJ 07417
www.careerpress.com
www.newpagebooks.com

Library of Congress Cataloging-in-Publication Data

Telesco, Patricia, 1960-
    Mastering candle magick : advanced spells and charms for every rite /
by Patricia Telesco.
        p. cm.
    Includes bibliographical references and index.
    ISBN 1-56414-654-5 (pbk.)
        1. Candles and lights—Miscellanea. 2. Magic. I. Title.

BF1623.C26 T46 2003
133.4'3--dc21

2002041090

Contents

Introduction

"Thousands of candles can be lighted from a single candle, and the life of the candle will not be shortened. Happiness never decreases by being shared."

—Buddha

I would go one step further to say that candlelight, when shared, *encourages* happiness and contentment. There is a special ambiance and magick in the glow of a candle, and it was recognized by one of our ancestors. As early as the 4th century B.C.E., human beings were lighting some form of candle to banish the darkness of night and the darkness of spirit that often surrounded them in a harsh world.

While our lives are not as difficult as theirs, they are certainly more complex. We also need that hopeful light— that glow, hope, and happiness that comes from a single taper lit with thoughtful intention. Thus, Candle Magick remains one of the oldest, most widely utilized, and most widely respected methods in the metaphysical world.

Mastering Candle Magick builds on the foundation established by our ancestors and contemporaries alike. Before the word "mastering" puts you off, however, let me explain that in the pages of this book this term denotes and promotes more of an attitude, outlook, and approach more than anything else. If we are walking our walk every moment of every day, our lives become an act of worship. From here, all else is simply icing on that proverbial cake (and in this case we get the candles, too!).

Some of you might be thinking that Candle Magick is by its very definition "low magick"—magick of the common people practiced in simple, functional, and sublime ways. You are correct! We need not reinvent the wheel here. If the method isn't broken—why fix it? There is no way I, or any author, could make Candle Magick any more approachable and adaptable than it is already. Instead, *Mastering Candle Magick* strives to give you sound constructs and fresh ideas for using traditional techniques in new and meaningful ways, specifically in combination with some of the emerging components and tools that technology provides for us.

Additionally, in the first book of this series we discussed using candles in specific settings—for divination, ritual, spellcraft, feng shui, charms, prayers, meditations, and astrology. Now we're going to take a slightly different tact and look at applying this wonderfully available and simple component/focus for everyday needs and goals. Are you tired of being in a dead end job? Are you looking for coven mates that share your magickal vision? Do you want to build spiritual kinships—a tribe with whom you feel wholly at home? Do you long for intimate, lasting companionship? All of these things, and many more, can be accomplished through the creative, willful, and determined application of Candle Magick.

But don't stop there. Include one other very important aspiration—your growth as a magickal person. It has been said that we are spiritual beings having a human experience. I believe that statement is true. In that context, each of us is a candle in our own right. Your soul is the candle's eternal wick, your heart, the flame. Your mind and your desire to learn are the air that gives it life, and your body is the wax. As you begin to understand this symbolism, you can burn ever more brightly and come closer to fulfilling your quest for enlightenment.

With that in mind, *Mastering Candle Magick* discusses the symbolic value of candles when connecting with our own souls, and with Spirit on an intimate level. It also shares ideas for creating your own candlelit spells or adapting those you find in this or any book so they're truly meaningful. By so doing, this book becomes a Candle Grimoire in every sense of the word, one to which you can turn again and again for constructs or inspiration.

So how does all this make our candle magick efforts "advanced?" Perhaps "advanced" is a poor choice of words. It's certainly not more complex, time consuming, or difficult than before. Rather, the idea here is mastering our practices and arts so they live outside the proverbial box. Advance them with your sincerity, your intensity, and your determination. Advance them based on your patience, creativity, and sensitivity. Candle Magick, like any spiritual method, advances as far and as fast as you allow it—as far and as quickly as you allow in your own spirit!

Let there be a light in the darkness.
Let our magick shine.
We put flame to wick,
And together, in the warmth of the candle's glow,
We begin....

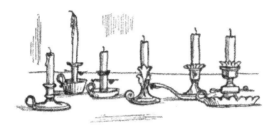

The Next Step

"*Acquaintance without patience is like a candle with no light.*"

—Iranian Proverb

Part One

Building on the Basics

"A candle loses nothing by lighting another candle. "

—Father James Keller

According to the dictionary, the root word for "advance" means to promote, bring to the forefront, furnish to others, enhance (or improve), and move forward. These definitions give us a fine place to start our journey through *Mastering Candle Magick*. As I mentioned in the introduction, "advanced" in this setting doesn't necessarily mean more complex, only a little more creative, insightful, and responsible. But let's take the definition one word at a time to illustrate.

Mastering Candle Magick promotes this ancient art by further establishing it as an accepted and adored metaphysical method, as well as a spiritual expression that has plenty of room for personalization and growth. Candle Magick came out of the warm and wise traditions of everyday folk. As opposed to the harshness of modern lighting, candles speak to us of less chaotic times. Their glow is comforting and hopeful, like the dawn. The process indicated for nearly all Candle Magick efforts is reasonably straightforward, and better still is the availability of the media. This combination makes Candle Magick appealing to both our ancestors and us!

Now, I am not one to recreate the wheel when the one I have works just fine. However, in the effort to promote the wheel of forward progression, I strongly advocate taking the best of what we have from Candle Magick's history and putting our own spin on it. Rather like leaving your fingerprint on a glass, taking the time to experiment and play with your media (namely candles) impresses them with your energy signature. This, in turn, leads to wholly unique and meaningful results (that is, your personal "spin" on the energy).

In terms of "bringing to the forefront," I want to stress that while Candle Magick is a simple art form, it can have sublime beauty. We need to raise the bar in how we perceive this ancient practice and not let the natural ease of the processes fool us into thinking that Candle Magick is any less powerful or practicable. The notion that fancy makes better is a very worldly one. Spiritually speaking, simplicity does not equate to wimpy results, and our ancestors were not foolish. If a process didn't yield results, then they didn't continue to utilize it. The simplicity is part of what endears Candle Magick to the heart of the most adept spiritual seekers. In our busy world, simple and functional is good!

Beyond this, magick has always been about creating changes. Because we face environments daily where transformations are needed or desired, our magickal methods need to be "brought to the forefront" of everyday life. Candles represent a beautiful way to achieve that goal without necessarily invoking images of Witches in pointy hats (I mean, how many people do you know personally who have candles in their house and do not practice magick?). This is very important for those practitioners who, because of personal circumstances, cannot be wholly out of their proverbial broom closet.

Finally, I write self-help books to furnish ideas that may enhance or improve each reader's experience. The whole purpose behind *Mastering Candle Magick* is one of exploring ways to add in, personalize, or enhance your candle-lighting efforts for any ritual, spell, charm, meditation or other metaphysical process. The ideas I'm presenting here are ones I've tried with a reasonable amount of success, but they're not being dolled out as dogma. As always, please trust in that small voice within to know what works best for you. I know I frequently say that, but it's a very important reminder, especially for newer practitioners who may feel a little uncertain. You truly do have the power to make and change your reality, but that magick only works if you trust your heart.

Speaking of trusting and trying, the experimentation process utilized for this book has confirmed that Candle Magick is among the most adaptable of all the Wise Crafts. Its components are easily obtained and inexpensive! The frugal, time-challenged Kitchen Witch in me sees this as the best of all worlds. You shouldn't have to go much further than your pantry or supermarket shelf to find the ingredients for every activity listed herein. And when you can't find the exact items, there are ideas for substitution included in each section. Which brings me to the next topic: how to adapt the candlelit spells you find in this or other books.

Adapting and Personalizing Prefabricated Candle Magick Spells:

"The best candle is understanding."

—Welsh Proverb

While it is certainly much easier on your schedule to use a prefabricated spell, the results aren't always as satisfying, especially if something seems amiss in the initial perusal. One step toward adeptness is being able to recognize when a process, or its components aren't quite right for your vision and path. Therefore, this section provides some guidelines by which to adapt and personalize candlelit spells so they manifest in the most successful and fulfilling way possible.

First, ask yourself what you feel the problem is with the spell. Is it the components, the symbolism, the wording, the focus? If the components are the issue (either because you don't have the ones recommended, or don't want to work with those items), that's one of the easiest things to fix. For example, if you don't have the suggested aromatic oil, use a good correspondence list such as the one provided in Appendix B to find another appropriate one. Putting this into a specific example, if you're fresh out of rose oil with which to anoint your candle in a love spell, you could use lavender, jasmine, vanilla, or violet (among many others) instead. Or if you happen to have rosewater in your pantry, that'd do the trick too!

What about components that modern practitioners no longer use, or those with which he or she may be unfamiliar? The same type of substitution holds true. It is, however, important that you fully understand the contextual purpose for the ingredient. If, for example, you read a spell that calls for dabbing the bottom of the candle with Treacle, the natural reaction from most folks would be, "What the heck is Treacle?" However, there's nothing wrong with Treacle, even if it sounds funny. That's just the old name for molasses and it makes an excellent component for symbolizing holding fast to an idea or goal. In this case, it was just a matter of doing a little research to fully appreciate the meaning of the original spell rather than actually needing to substitute anything. Don't have molasses? How about glue or bubble gum?

The example of molasses brings me to an important point that cannot be stressed enough no matter how advanced the practitioner or the process. Meaningfulness is nothing less than essential in magick. While it might be a little time-consuming to discern the meanings of oddly-spelled, older words, if you don't understand what you're supposed to use and why, you won't be able to find a suitable substitute, and/or the spell **WILL NOT** work for you. There's no mental connection to the process or the symbols, and therefore it will produce no energy.

Similarly (and this may sound a bit militant), if you're going through the motions just to impress someone—stop right now! Magick is between you and Spirit, and you and your heart. If you do anything that breaks personal ideals or taboos, any stray magick that might be created is likely to go awry anyway!

Speaking of taboos, there are the old spells that include unacceptable ingredients by modern standards. For example, many of the ancient Grimoires include spells that call for blood because it was considered a very personal and very powerful component. Now, in our health-conscious times, avoiding that ingredient is sensible. In this case, look to a couple of alternatives such as saliva, or, if wishing for a color correspondence, tomato juice. The saliva compares well to blood as a personal bodily fluid; The tomato juice corresponds in texture and color.

The important thing in all cases of adaptation is that you maintain continuity of the symbolic value. So, if you have issues with the symbols used in a spell, change them, but make sure your changes make sense. Let's say the spell's instructions call for carving an upward-pointing arrow to represent an increase of energy. You, however, prefer the mathematical sign for "greater than" ($>$). The solution is simple. Carve the mathematical sign on the candle instead.

It still maintains the basic value of all parts of the spell, but means more to *you* when you look at it.

Next, we consider the wording. Let's face it, very few of today's practitioners are comfortable with Shakespearean style prose. I'm not sure I'm ready for a Rap style invocation either (but that's just me). Read over any verbal components and say them out loud. Does anything stick on your tongue or feel completely foreign? Those are the words and phrases you should seriously consider changing. Focus is everything in spellcraft, and if you're worrying over your words, you have less energy to give to results.

This is also a good time to mention any spells that include words in foreign languages. I highly suggest you either have a working knowledge of that language, or someone who can teach you the correct pronunciation, before using any such incantation. Incorrect inflection, tone, or pronunciation can dramatically change the meanings of some foreign words and phrases. Unless you *enjoy* completely uncontrolled surprises in your spellcraft, know what you're saying and how to say it, or substitute words from your native tongue!

This brings up a good point for readers for whom English is a second language. If you are more comfortable using Spanish, French, or German—translate your spells into that language. Our minds react to language in very specific ways; Words do, indeed, have power. There is absolutely no reason not to work with a linguistic construct with which you're familiar, and have greater understanding.

What about the spell's focus? I know that sounds odd, but I've read some very well-constructed ancient spells that I would **never** consider using for the purpose for which they were designed. For example, one spell says to put a nail in the footprint of an enemy to cause him or her harm (probably somewhat similar to using a poppet). While the White Witch in me recoils at such a dark deed, the symbolic value really grabs my attention. To adapt this concept to Candle Magick, I'd suggest pushing a nail through a candle while reciting an incantation, and then letting the candle burn to that point (akin to having an X that marks the spot where the magick really takes flight).

USEFUL IDEAS FOR SPELL ADAPTATION AND CREATION

* Rather than using one candle, use several arranged in a symbolic pattern.

* Make Candle Magick a group effort with each person bringing and lighting a significant candle.

* Move with a candle through a pattern (literally putting your magick into action) or move other items around the candle to create the pattern of power.

* As you light the candle, remember your purpose; As you put it out, it signals closure for the spell, but the energy keeps moving.

* Turn candles clockwise in their base a symbolic number of times to generate positive "spin," and counterclockwise for banishing.

* Turn the candle over and light the bottom to, likewise, "turn" the energy.

* Melt the candle completely for banishing. This provides the visual impact of the unwanted energies disappearing.

* If you're going to be doing a lot of Candle Magick, seriously consider buying a small portable fire extinguisher. Accidents do happen; Safety first applies to magick, too!

※ Divide the candle into sections for units of time (they should be equidistant, but need not be perfectly clocked). Burn a symbolic number of units of the candle that reflect your goal (see Appendix B for numerical correspondences). This is reminiscent of how candle clocks were once made, and I actually advocate using a candle clock to mark quality time with others whom you care about. While the candle burns, they are your primary focus and the candlelight encourages a relaxed atmosphere in which to nourish relationships. This is also a good way to mark weekly meditative time.

※ If you freeze a candle first, lighting it helps "warm" things (a symbol particularly useful in love and relationship spells) and it burns longer.

※ Alter your chosen candle's shape and aroma so that both symbolize the circumstance and need.

※ Shape some wax around a wick into an image of what you hope to achieve using the law of sympathy to guide you (this is especially useful in banishings where burning the image makes it disappear). Sympathy simply means "like attracts like" and it is the theory behind poppet-making as well.

※ Use feng shui to help choose a suitable location for your candle (see *Exploring Candle Magick,* New Page Books 2001). Alternatively, place them in an elemental quarter: Earth for mundane matters like money and grounding, Water for emotional matters, Fire for energy and purification, and Air for communication and creativity.

※ Make your own candles when possible. You can time their creation and design the preparation process so they can better reflect your goals.

❄ Layer the colors in hand-dipped candles so that each layer burned represents part of the magickal process. For example, in Prosperity Magick, make the outside layer brown for firm foundations, and then the inside layer green. This creates a strong base in which your money can grow.

❄ Knot the wick of your candle, binding wishes or energy inside the knot so its released when burning.

❄ Chose the base of your candle so it also represents your goal by its shape, color, or decorative patterns.

❄ Consider working your Candle Magick in sacred space (see Step 7, page 32).

❄ Create a special candle storage box where your tools will not get chipped or bent from heat. For protection, line it with a soft cloth which can also be used to polish the wax. If you have separate boxes for each color, you can also add dried herbs or essential oil beneath the cloth (over time the candles absorb the aroma and energy of the herbs or oil chosen).

❄ Think of an incantation that you can use when you blow out a candle that keeps the magick moving forward nonetheless. For example (to ease tension in the home):

"While the light is gone, the wish remains.
Let peace fall on this house again."

As you can see, the process of adapting prefabricated spells isn't that difficult. If you think of the process as analogous to baking a cake, you'll have a firm grasp of the approach. You can't randomly substitute a component in this "recipe" that doesn't mix well with the whole. We can't add more of a specific energy signature than prescribed without having the entire magickal cake fall flat, or be completely off balance in the way it manifests. Basically, just take some time and think it through, being aware that you might have to try more than one time to mix it just right! Practice still makes perfect, even in (and perhaps especially in) metaphysics.

Creating Your Own Candle Magick Spells

*"If you have knowledge,
let others light their candles in it."*

—Margaret Fuller

Another big step toward spiritual growth along your magickal Path is to begin creating your own spells, but plenty of practitioners I meet feel uncertain about that. Their reasons vary. They may not know traditional spell constructs, or they may feel insecure in their own ability. This section is designed to give either group of people the confidence to take what they can learn from the history of spellcraft in terms of constructs, and apply it to wholly new creations that sing the song of their souls!

Before you say, *"I can't do that, I'm not an expert,"* I'll let you in on a secret: You don't become an expert over night, and sometimes not even in a lifetime. Someone somewhere had to devise the first love spell, healing spell, crop growth spell, and so forth. Then more people came along and created spells that made sense in their historical-cultural setting. This ongoing process of invention is truly a legacy on which modern practitioners can draw quite readily once we accept the role of being our own Priest or Priestess.

Ah, is that pair of shoes a little too uncomfortable to try on, even more so than making your own spells? Relax.

You already assume this role in your life every day when you make moral or ethical choices. In those moments you are the guru and guide for your life. All you'll be doing now is activating that capacity more fully (which is exactly what an adept strives to do 24 hours a day, seven days a week).

As with adapting prefabricated spells, this process is going to take a little serious consideration, but don't be dissuaded. I can promise you the time and effort you put forth will not only result in an improved understanding of and an improved success rate with your spells, but in all magickal methods. This is because magick is akin to a web. Most methods touch upon each other in some manner or another, and the remaining ones actually work together with each other. For example, you often hear the word "meditation" followed by the phrase "and visualization." This is because the two techniques compliment each other. The same principle applies to spellcraft! You'll find the basic schematics that you learn and utilize repeatedly often help in creating more successful rituals, amulets, potions, etc.

The Process:

In reading over numerous books, both modern and ancient, there seems to be 10 readily identifiable steps in the spell creation process. Now, I'm sure you can find people who disagree, or who do it differently. That's perfectly natural in a vision-driven faith, but we have to start somewhere, so look at this list as a rough black-and-white outline to which you bring the crayons of your experience and imagination:

Step One: *Determine your goal.* Quite simply, you can't bake the cake without knowing what kind of cake you want! And it doesn't stop there. What about the size, the shape, the toppings? Using this analogy, it's easy to see why I strongly suggest thinking about your spell's goal(s) in detail. Perhaps you want to design a love spell. What type of love do you seek? Do you want romance, longevity, just a playful fling? Be specific here or the universe will interpret things for you (trust me). A great illustration of this came from a person who contrived a companionship spell that included things such as hair color, eye color, and personality. She left out one minor detail, however: species. Her perfect companion (which came to her shortly after the spell, and fitted the entire description perfectly) was a dog! In this manner, magick is similar to a computer program—it does exactly what you tell it to do; no more and no less. When you leave out some instructional language, however, the results get very interesting!

Some other things to consider at this time are the potential permutations of your goal. This is where we get into ethics. Is what you want manipulative or harmful? If so, are you ready and willing to accept all the karmic implications of what you're about to do? If not, I'd advise setting aside magick and opting for old-fashioned mundane efforts to rectify the situation on your own.

Once you have a detailed overview of your goal, and feel secure in your motivations, proceed to step two.

Step Two: *Choose Components and symbols to represent that goal.* Okay, some readers are probably sitting there saying, *"Well this is a Candle Magick book, so beyond the candles, what else can be included in Candle Magick?"* The answer to that question is that nearly everything can (everything, that is, that supports the goal in its symbolic value and metaphysical associations). You can play inspiring music while you work, add movement, dab on aromatics, and burn incense. Use any manner of props to illustrate your goal, and even include special timing *(see Appendix B)*.

I like to make a list of all the items that I think might be useful for the spell I have in mind, and then choose the items that are both available and really meaningful to me from that list. When you do this, please don't limit this brain storming to just items found on various traditional correspondence lists. Rather, include those things that come immediately to mind when you think about your core theme. For example, when contriving a spell to improve your mood or sense of humor, perhaps feathers pop into your mind (They tickle one's fancy!). When designing a spell for communication, a telephone may similarly inspire you. See, it doesn't matter that neither of these items were necessarily located on any conventional list of components because the symbolic value is completely obvious to *you*, and you're the one casting the spell! This returns to the notion of being your own Priest or Priestess. Start trusting those instincts if you haven't already!

Step Three: *Making a Blueprint*: This step comes somewhat under the "chicken and the egg" discussion. If you don't have a design in mind for your spell, it's hard to choose components and if you don't know what components you have available (or prefer) it's hard to make a design! Nonetheless, its generally easier to pattern magick when you have determined the focal points and props. You can now start thinking more like a director thinks; the spell is a play through which you're illustrating your will for the universe.

Taking this staged metaphor further, every play has a beginning, middle, and end. Throughout the action, everything that happens is leading to a distinct point. In this case, the progression of the spell from beginning to end must be designed to build energy and then release it toward your goal. Let's use job hunting as an illustration. When you're trying to find work, the first thing that needs to happen is to discover the right leads. Perhaps part of your spell would include dabbing some rosemary oil on the want ads so that your conscious mind's awareness is heightened while reading (this is where your props come in). To this foundation, lighting a candle makes sense (shining a light on things).

The next part of the spell might be to take the ads that jumped out at you, and reciting an incantation over them before you make calls or mail resumes. All the while the candle continues to burn. In fact if you have 7-day candles that can be kept safely burning until you succeed, even better! Many times interview prospects and call backs come within a week's time. Do you see how the progression is logically based on normal human patterns? That's very important. Magick should work with Nature, not against it.

The progression should also make logical sense in terms of the goal. When you're trying to lessen or banish something, the items that represent that "something" shouldn't *grow* during the spell (making a burning candle the ideal media). In all, just remember that these blueprints you're designing say something specific to your subconscious and super conscious self, the Collective Unconscious, and Spirit. They fashion the way in which your energy manifests. Lay out a couple of potential approaches and then look at them as a whole, picking the one that seems really right for your mind and spirit.

Step Four: *Verbal or Written Materials.* In step two and three it's easy to see where some type of written or verbalized charm, incantation, or invocation might be appropriate to your goals. If this turns out to be the case, and you want that type of element included, write one! Bear in mind that worded components need not be rhymed, eloquent or long to be effective. In fact, plenty of old charms were very short ditties that people could easily remember. One that comes to mind is:

> *"Leaf of ash I do thee pluck*
> *to bring to me a day of luck."*

No great literary piece, for sure, but it states the goal clearly and the most common of person could remember it (rather like a commercial jingle!).

Having said that, there are very specific items to consider in your wording. First, always use terms that you wholly understand and can easily memorize. If you're stumbling over an incantation, it increases the likelihood of loosing your spiritual focus. Second, rhyme may sound a little hokey, but it helps the mnemonic process for those who have trouble remembering things (especially in a pinch). Third, the meter of a worded component can carry symbolism that supports the goal of the spell. For example, a standard 4/4 beat represents the Earth Element and foundations (the four corners of creation). Therefore, it might be ideal to use this cadence when writing an incantation for a prosperity spell (Earthly matters). Better still, use a drum to sound out the 4/4 beat and your wishes while the candle burns (the sound of the drum represents Earth's rhythms as they blend with your heartbeat and will!).

Phrases that comes up a lot in verbal and written components are "for the greatest good" or "for the good of all." These phrases are what I consider a karmic catchall. While no one would want to accidentally harm another or cause more problems than good, we have a limited amount of perspective in our humanity. By including this type of wording in your spells, you acknowledge the part of the picture (the Web of Life) that you cannot possibly see and can ask the Universe to step in with guidance, should it need to. I personally have never felt so adept in my spellcraft or so wise in my spirit as to leave this clause out of my workings!

Perhaps something happens that you can't use a planned verbal component (like privacy restrictions). Quite simply, THINK! The mind is where magick begins, and your thoughts are every bit as powerful as words. Close your eyes and recite your incantation inwardly with as much conviction as you would out loud, and then continue with the spell as planned.

Step Five: *Proper Personal Preparation*. You're done with all the fussing in terms of choosing your components and laying out the blueprint for your spell. What's left, other than casting it? Getting yourself in the right frame of mind for magick. No matter how advanced the practitioner is, weariness, worries, sickness, and other of life's normal negatives will interfere with your magick, usually in a not-so-nice way. Little bits of that energy seep into what you're creating because *you* enable the process. It amazes me how many people go through the motions of a spell feeling awful and then wonder why they get awful results! It's "like attracting like" on a very intimate level. Approach Candle Magick as you would any other sacred task and you'll fare well.

Setting aside the negatives, however, let's assume that your mind, body, and spirit are all in the right space for magick. What other types of preparations can you make so that you're wholly focused? My personal preferences are minimally a few moments of quiet introspection. If time allows, meditation and prayer also really help direct my concentration to exactly where it needs to be (and where it needs to remain throughout the spell). A meditative, prayerful demeanor seems to open my spirit to both giving and receiving, thereby enhancing the overall flow of energies.

Mind you, this is only what works best for *me*. *You* are a unique spiritual being, and therefore you may have to find a completely different approach. I know people who enjoy taking baths, anoint themselves, listen to music, dance to sacred songs, or take a long walk (a moving meditation) before spellcraft. Each of these actions becomes a tool that helps us bridge the gap between the temporal and metaphysical, and connects us mentally and spiritually with the process, while also improving concentration. My best advice is to try different methods and then do a self-check afterward to see which one leaves you feeling the most balanced and focused. Finding sound, magickal processes that really work for you are well worth your time.

Step Six: *Preparing Ingredients.* Once you're fully prepared for the work ahead, do the same for all the props and ingredients that are going to take part in the spell. Items that have been sitting around your house, being handled by many people, will collect energy, not all of which is beneficial to your magickal process. So it makes perfect sense to purify these items and then charge them for the purpose at hand.

Cleansing can take many forms. You can visualize pure, silver-white light pouring into the item until it feels warm, smudge the item with cedar or sage incense, or even wash it with spring water. The idea is to eliminate any random patterns that could influence the magick adversely.

Charging, for those of you who are not familiar with it, is a little different. Now that the items in question are spiritually empty its time to fill them with the appropriate magick! There are several ways to accomplish this. You can energize the components by sunlight or moonlight for a significant number of minutes (sunlight stresses the masculine, conscious processes, while moonlight stresses the feminine and intuitive processes). Another option is that you can place your hands, palm downward, over the components and think of your purpose, letting energy flow from you into the components (a visualization often helps here).

A third way to charge your candles is by dressing them. "Dressing" means anointing the candle with a symbolic aromatic oil, working from middle toward both ends. This action also designates its purpose if the color of the candle is not correct (or generic), or if you wish to slightly adjust the color's symbolic value for an alternative symbolism. For example, if you want a friendly love but the only colored candle you have is a bright red (the color of heated passion) you can tone down the energy by using an aromatic more suited to amiable feelings (sweet pea or lemon comes to mind). In this manner, the type of dressing reflects the candle's purpose in your spell. If the candle represents you or another person, the dressing should likewise vibrate with the energies of that individual (perhaps by using personal perfume or cologne rather than oils). Similarly, if the candle is an offering to a deity, if it represents the day of the week (of the spellcasting), or an astrological energy, the dressing should be chosen accordingly.

Step Seven: *Preparing the Environment*: Before we even begin discussing magickal preparations, first consider the pragmatics of your surroundings. Where, exactly, can you put your candles and components so they're safe and away from flimsy curtains, other flammable items, stray hands, or paws and whiskers? This question also brings to bear a second—do you want or need an altar space on which to set everything up? Having an altar may resolve the safety issues, but a "formal" altar isn't necessary. Any flat, stable surface will do. Remember, sacredness is more about attitude than platitudes, and not everyone can keep a formal altar erected all the time.

Another thing to consider is the overall working conditions. If there's a lot of movement in your spell, you'll want to be sure that windows are closed (so candles don't get blown out) and that the floor is free of clutter. And don't forget to check your own clothing in this consideration process. I can't tell you how many times I've seen very lovely, flowing dresses catch on fire when someone went to light an altar candle adjacent to those already burning. We want the *magick* to be hot—not the practitioners!

Once you've found a good location where you can work and hopefully not get interrupted in the middle of things (which would mess up most people's focus), the next question is that of creating sacred space. Because Candle Magick is considered an elementary process (Folk Magick), it is not absolutely necessary to invoke the Quarters (or Watchtowers) for your spellcasting. Nonetheless if you have the time, it certainly won't hurt anything. Sacred space not only protects you from unwanted influences but also holds your energy in place until you're ready to move it outward and direct it. Rather like a plug in a spiritual sink, this will keep stray bits of energy from flowing out before you've completed the desired pattern.

Many traditions have a specific way of erecting the sacred Circle. Many solitaries have their own approaches. For those readers who have neither on which to draw, I'd like to take a moment and share some ideas should you choose to cast your spell within a Circle.

First, think of sacred space like a sphere of energy that surrounds you in all directions while you work. You can visualize this like a sparkling white bubble or something similar if it helps. To create this sphere of energy, Witches and many Neo-Pagans call on the powers associated with the four corners of creation—namely Earth, Air, Fire, and Water. In the center of this Circle the practitioner and Spirit reside.

To invoke these energies, stand in the direction in which each resides and invite them to join your magickal moment. Earth is due North, Air is East, Fire is South, and Water is West. You can do this in any respectful manner you choose. Here's an example that begins in the East (the place where the sun rises, symbolizing the start of our magick). Just make sure you have all your components set out and ready to go before you take this step, and that they're all within the sphere you're creating:

Turn to the East and say:

> *"From the East I call the Air,*
> *Come and with you magick bear."*

Turn to the South and say:

> *"From the South I call the Fire,*
> *Come and move the magick higher."*

Turn to the West and say:

> *"From the West I call the Rain,*
> *Come and nourish my spirit again."*

Turn to the North and say:

> *"From the North I call the Earth,*
> *Come and to the magick give birth!"*

As you can see, this isn't overly difficult to remember, nor is it fancy. As you call on each power, focus on the energies involved. If you wish, add a symbolic element into the invocation like waving a feather in the Air at the East, or burning some incense in the South. This honors the Natural powers on which you're calling for assistance.

When you've completed the Circle, go to the center and welcome Spirit in whatever words feel right to you. If you're working with a specific god or goddess, this is a good time to mention that Being by name, and put something on the altar to represent that presence. In Candle Magick, a white or a gold candle is ideal for a god, and a silver candle for a goddess (unless they have a colors associated with them already).

Step Eight: *Building & Releasing the Magick.* At last it's time to start making magick. Follow the blueprint you created in step three, making sure to maintain your focus throughout the spellcasting process. As you follow the spell step-by-step, you should feel the air begin to tingle with energy. Alternatively, some people hear a humming, and others still smell a change in the air. Usually your senses will give you some indication that you're doing it right.

The defining moment of the spell comes when you release it. You have all this energy created for a purpose, but akin to an arrow just sitting knocked in a bow, it won't do much good until you let it fly. Some people indicate this motion physically (by pointing or raising their arms). Other people use a particular action in the spell as a cue (such as a pinned candle burning down to that point and the pin falling out). Whatever you choose, continue your focus and begin guiding the energy as far out as you can, to your spiritual event horizon. From that point forward you must trust in your construct and the energies raise to manifest for the greatest good.

This is also the juncture at which many practitioners release their sacred space. This is easily done by simply reversing the earlier process discussed, and saying farewell to the energies. Here's an example of wording for your reference:

Turn to the North saying:

> *"Return to the North, return o' Earth,*
> *and thank you for your protective presence."*

Turn counterclockwise to the West saying:

> *"Return to the West, return o' Water,*
> *and thank you for your protective presence."*

Turn counterclockwise again to the South saying:

> *"Return to the South, return o' Fires,*
> *and thank you for your protective presence."*

Turn to the East and say:

> *"Return to the East, return o' Winds,*
> *and thank you for your protective presence."*

When you've finished this widdershins dismissal, it's an excellent time to thank Spirit and blow out the Spirit candle on your altar if one was used. Put away any components that should not be left out (such as a candle that needs to stay burning) until next time.

Step Nine: *Grounding and Ongoing Focus.* Magick is hard work and it often leaves people a little out of sorts. The best way to combat this off-center feeling is by grounding. Either sit down close to the earth, put your fingers in some sand or soil, hold a bit of obsidian, eat something crunchy such as carrots (a root vegetable), or have an old fashioned hamburger! All of these actions help ground out excess energy and return you to a normal level of awareness. But wait— your work isn't done yet!

Creating and casting a spell is but one part of a much bigger picture. Now, you need to support your magick in word and deed. Follow up on your goals mundanely (this is part of being a co-creator), and periodically reinforce your spell until it manifests. This is not a lack of faith on your part. Each time you add energy into a spell, a sturdier bridge is created between the worlds over which your will can travel more easily. Reinforcement also stresses and clarifies the specifics of your goal even further.

Light up my Life: Integrating Spirituality and Spirit

"We say God and the imagination are one...How high that highest candle lights the dark."

—Wallace Stevens

Third in the trinity for soulful advancement (after adapting and personalizing prefabricated spells and creating your own spells) is the ability to focus on our spiritual nature. It has been said before that we are spiritual beings looking for a human experience. That humanness includes an amazing capacity to grow beyond our perceived limitations, including mystical ones. While such a discussion could become quite lofty, it really boils down to walking one's walk versus solely practicing the methodology (going through the motions). It also means connecting with the God and Goddess in an intimate way every moment of every day. Candle Magick can become a helpmate in that process.

To understand the candle's role in helping us with these goals, first let's consider the symbolism of the candle as it spanned both Western and Eastern philosophies and religions. The word candle means "to make bright." The early church took this to heart, often using candles not only for ambiance during services, but also as a representation of God or Christ's purity. Buddhism likens candlelight to the soulful power within each of us—power that we can tap into in order to move out of spiritual darkness and achieve enlightenment. In this system, by lighting the candle, we light our spirit, intentionally leaving behind the mundane/temporal world in favor of the magickal/eternal.

Now, while all that sounds very nice, you might be wondering how to go about actually putting these ideas into practice. One suggestion I have is that of a daily god or goddess candle. I keep at least one candle on my altar all the time. Each day when I get up, I mindfully light that taper and welcome Spirit into my day. I may not spend more than a moment here saying "hello" but it's an important moment nonetheless. It would be so easy to go through the day routinely and forget about the Divine, but that's not the way spiritual seekers should live. We must be mindful, and in our mindfulness—act. This small daily routine keeps me mindful and provides an action that literally ignites a prayerful, grateful attitude.

If you find morning devotions don't work for you (not everyone is a "morning person"), how about one at dinner? For most people, this is the one time of the day when rushing stops for a few moments. We sit and gather our thoughts or our family together and enjoy a good meal. In part, that's why mealtime prayers were popular for a very long time. Lighting a candle at dinner can become your mindful prayer and action (If you live with others you may wish to take turns so everyone's involved).

Another possibility would be to allow for some pre-sleep meditation and reflection. Light a candle (I suggest a safety conscious, self-enclosed one just in case you fall asleep) and think about your day. Ask yourself if the Divine provided any nudges or guidance, and if so what those moments meant to you. Be thankful for your blessings, and then blow out the candle so you can sleep with joy and Spirit in your heart.

As you can see, these types of activities aren't overly time-consuming or fancy. The point is that you're making a space for the Divine in your life (not that S/he ever really left, it's only our focus that's been wanting). Spirit is always here—in us, around us, above us, below us, throughout the universe and dimensions. It's normal to loose sight of that at various junctures in our lives, but when you're seeking adepthood it's important to recapture that vision and awareness. To start off on the right foot, if you can take a moment right now and light a candle in a special location. Think of it as a symbol of your inner light, growing into fullness. Let it become the light in the darkness, reaching ever outward to the Goddess and God—the ultimate Light of reason, magick, fulfillment, and wholeness, then just BE.

What to Expect

"Common sense is the wick of the candle."

—Ralph Waldo Emerson

What kind of results can you expect from Candle Magick? Quite honestly, for such a simple method I've seen some pretty impressive manifestations. Plenty here depends on *you*. How much focus you give the spell, how much support you provide afterward, and how much you trust in your magick all influence the results. Additionally, if you include the karmic catchall phrase (*and it harm none* or *for the greatest good*), the lack of results or delayed results come from a necessity predicated by the part of the "big picture" you didn't see.

I realize this seems like a non-answer, but it's the most honest one. Anyone who tells you that a magickal process will absolutely work perfectly (perfect, in this case, meaning exactly as you anticipate) 100 percent of the time is a charlatan. Magick is not now, nor has it ever been, a perfect art. There are too many variables to make that kind of statement. Nonetheless, I do believe Candle Magick is a very viable tool for your alchemical kit, and that you'll find it a very satisfying. With that said, let's move forward together and explore some sample spells to which you can bring your imagination and creativity for personally meaningful and positive results.

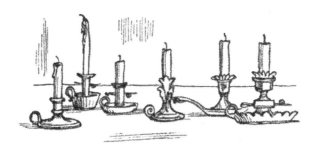

Putting Match to Wick

"Religion is a candle inside a multicolored lantern. Everyone looks through a particular color, but the candle is always there."

—Mohammed Naguib

Part Two

 # Spells, Charms, Rituals, and Divinations

*"If you have knowledge,
let others light their candles at it."*

—Margaret Fuller

This part of the book provides several examples of Candle Magick for a wide variety of themes. This way when you need a magical method for love, health, peace, forgiveness, or whatever, you have a construct from which to begin. These constructs are only there are helpmates, not edicts. In fact, each prototype also includes advantageous times to cast the spell and potential alternative components to allow for greater personalization and flexibility. View the construct like a black and white outline, the alternatives as crayons, and then have some fun!

Note that the topics/themes in this part are listed alphabetically. If you don't find a theme that quite suits what you had in mind, try a synonym. For example, if prosperity wasn't listed you could try abundance, money, or wealth (depending, of course, on what area of your life you wish to prosper—a prosperous garden would more likely be listed under "gardening").

I trust that you will find this a helpful and creative guide to all your candle magick efforts.

Abundance

The linguistical root of the word abundance means "and wave." Putting this into modern vernacular, abundant energy is like a swelling tide to the point of overflowing. With that in mind, this theme represents an opportunity to mingle Fire and Water energies into your spellcraft. Beyond this blend, efforts aimed at abundance are best supported when you:

※ Time your spells for the waxing to full moon, the season of Spring, or dawn.

※ Add aromatics such as sandalwood, ginger, or vanilla.

※ Use green candles (for growth), blue candles (for the "wave"), or gold or yellow candles (solar energy).

※ Include other potential components and symbols like yellow apples, berries, seeds, and anything that reminds you of profuseness.

Spells

For this first spell you'll need seven light green candles (the color of new growth). You'll also need something that symbolizes the area of your life to which you wish to bring abundance. Put the symbol in the middle of a sturdy table. Starting on the day of a waxing moon, place one candle adjacent to the emblem and light it. As you set match to this candle say:

> "Over seven days, this light shall shine;
> Come the 8th abundance will be mine!"

Leave this to burn for a few minutes while you focus your attention on the symbol, then blow it out to release your prayer. On day two, put the second candle clockwise to the right of the first, then light the first and second candles (in clockwise order), repeating the incantation twice. Follow this process in kind on days three through seven.

On day eight, the candles surround the symbol in a circle (representing completion). After lighting the candles take them to eight places throughout the house (to spread abundance) and let them naturally burn out. The symbol can be buried if it's biodegradable (so the energy is nourished and grows) or it can be kept in a safe place until the spell manifests.

❧ ༄ ⚘ ༄ ❧

For this spell you'll need a gold or yellow candle, a yellow apple, a pinch of ginger, one-half teaspoon. Vanilla, and a pat of butter. Slice the apple thinly across the width so that you can see the natural pentagram on every slice. Put this in a greased oven pan, sprinkling the slices evenly with the ginger and vanilla and breaking up the pat of butter over top. When you're done, rub a little of the ginger and vanilla on the candle, then light it saying:

> "By this blessed candle's light,
> abundance in every bite!
> This apple I bake for abundance sake."

Put the candle near the stove (but not so close that it melts). Bake the apple mixture at 300 degrees for about 20 minutes until it's golden brown and tender. Cool and perhaps drizzle with sweet cream (to encourage life's sweetness). Consume expectantly.

❧ ༄ ⚘ ༄ ❧

Gather together a drip-less candle (your choice of colors), some potting soil and a plant dish, a corn kernel (you can get seeds at any gardening shop) and a little water. Wait until the moon is in the waxing to full stage. (Alternatively, wait until the Moon is in Taurus. Astrological almanacs will contain this information.) Name the kernel after the area of your life that needs improved abundance. Place the seed purposefully in the soil. Add a little water, then secure the candle over top, using the soil as the "holder." Light the candle and repeat this incantation three times (to improve the body-mind-spirit connection):

"The seed of abundance I sow, in rich soil to grow.
By the wick and the flame, abundance I claim!"

Let this candle burn until it's very close to the soil, then remove the candle and tend to the plant with loving care. By the time the kernel sprouts, you should begin to see a turn-around.

Anger

The emotion of anger is one that leaves us out of balance. It can also be detrimental to magickal efforts because you can send out energy that you didn't intend (or minimally from which you really didn't want the karmic kickback). Therefore, the spells for anger are aimed at re-establishing self-control, and calming down so that anger doesn't blind.

- ※ Time your spells for the waning moon (so anger shinks), Winter (for cool clarity), moon in Aries (overcoming barriers), and moon in Gemini (balance or banishing).
- ※ Add aromatics such as lavender, pennyroyal, and violet (all of which promote peace).
- ※ Use blue or white candles (the traditional color for tranquility and harmony).
- ※ Include other potential components and symbols such as amethyst (promotes self-control), coral (to quell anger), water (puts out anger's fire), lotus (for spiritual equilibrium), or anything that reminds you of calmness.

Spells

For this spell you'll need to make a special ice cube and have a candle handy (your choice of color). Take a small plastic container and fill it two-thirds of the way with water and put it in your freezer. When it gets to soft-slush stage, insert your candle in the middle then let it finish freezing all the way. This way the ice becomes the candle's foundation for the spell.

When the ice is completely hard, take the container out and place it on a flat surface (your altar is one good choice). Light the candle saying:

"By my will and this spell, this anger shall quell.
The anger I felt, like this ice, it now melts."

Imagine pouring all your anger into the candle, and watch the ice. When it begins to melt, remove the candle for safety reasons and blow it out. Lay it beside the ice. When the ice is melted completely throw both away (to likewise put away your anger).

For this spell, you'll need to wait until the moon is waning. You'll also need two candles, one of which represents you and the other of which represents the person or situation toward which the anger exists. (Choose your colors accordingly and carve an emblem into each to signify their designation.) Put the two candles at opposite ends of a table. On the first night (at dusk, which marks an ending) light them saying:

"The light glows with reason and wisdom.
Let anger burn away and decrease; let there be peace."

Let the candle burn for 10 minutes (the number that stresses rationality). On the second night, move the two candles slightly closer together repeating the incantation and letting them burn again. Don't forget to focus on both yourself and the person or situation toward which the energy is directed. Continue this process until the night of the dark moon, when both candles should be allowed to burn for one hour (the number for cooperation) then extinguished together. Dispose of the candles as they represent your anger.

                    ✲ ⟨⟨⟩⟩ ✲

This spell calls for any type of first aid cream (as a key component) along with your candle, an amethyst crystal, and a few drops of aromatic oil (I chose lavender). Mix a few drops of the lavender oil into a small amount (less than one-half tea-spoon is more than enough) of the cream. Stir counter clock-wise saying:

> *"Anger shall wane, let there be peace again."*

Rub a little of this cream on the candle and the amethyst stone. Light the candle and place both it and the amethyst in a sunny window (so that the light of reason can shine on the situation). *Please make sure all curtains are firmly pulled back and the candle is secure.* Let the candle go out naturally, rinse off the crystal then carry it with you to encourage balance and harmony.

Authority

> *"Go within every day and find the inner strength so that the world will not blow your candle out."*
>
> —Katherine Dunham

I know there have been many times in my life when I wished I had a greater sense of jurisdiction and influence over a situation, and I'm sure I'm not alone. Spells for authority encourage this reliable demeanor (Note: Self-confidence is handled under spells for independence, to banish fear, etc.). Additionally, other spells that come under this category help you to better deal with authority figures with whom you're having troubles.

- ❋ Time your spells for noon (the sun represents authority and leadership), or when the moon is in Leo (to develop new skills and strength).
- ❋ Add aromatics: ginger (increased energy), cinnamon (protection from an adversarial authority figure), rose (improved awareness), lily of the valley (clear mindedness), and sage (wisdom).
- ❋ Use red candles (the traditional color for power), or white (to encourage rapport and peace with an authority figure).
- ❋ Include other potential components and symbols such as tea or thyme (courage), clover (trust), rowan wood (power and insight), and peaches (wisdom).

Spells

This first spell is designed to help you develop an improved sense of authority (Note: The authority must be in an area for which you *deserve* this authority otherwise it's abusing power). Pick out a candle that will represent *you* in this spell. Put it in a good holder on a flat surface, which has been covered by a piece of waxed paper. Surround the candle base with dry black tea. Light the candle at 11 a.m. saying this incantation three times:

"As this wax melts, let my influence be felt."

While that burns, gather up the tea and simmer it in warm water. Strain and bless the tea saying:

"Authority within, let the magick begin!"

Drink the tea to internalize the spell, then blow out the candle. You can reuse this for any spell pertaining to authority, strength, or bravery.

This spell helps you cope with a difficult authority figure. I used it once when I was working in an office where the supervisor for the secretaries was unusually critical of everyone. For it, you'll need a white candle and a poppet that has somehow been decorated to represent the person in question. For example, if the individual is a secretary, you could attach a pen or other office implement to the poppet. Now, you'll want to split your time on the candle burning portion of the spell, dividing it equally between noon and dusk so that you have symbolic value of sound reasoning combined with an ending (in this case to animosity). Place the candle and the poppet near each other. When you light it at noon say:

> *"Let there be honesty, respect,*
> *and clarity between me and thee."*

Let the candle burn half way down. On the same day, light it at dusk saying:

> *"Animosity be gone; let us learn to get along."*

Let the candle burn the remainder of the way down. Keep a small bit of the wax with you whenever you're in contact with that individual to keep the magick moving and close at hand!

Balance

> *"Better to light one small candle than to curse the*
> *darkness."*

> —Chinese Proverb

The yin-yang symbol is one of the best I know that illustrates ideal balance because it represents light in the darkness, the temporal in the immortal, the magick in the mundane, the feminine in the masculine, and so forth. True balance lies in recognizing these things and in honoring that symmetry somehow. Be that as it may, most of us rarely find complete equalization in our lives, let alone any one part at a time! The goal for balance spells, therefore, is to reestablish stability, neutrality, equilibrium, and even-handedness where it's most needed at the time.

※ Time your spells for noon or midnight (the in-between hours). Alternatively New Year's or Beltane are also good choices (both representing the transformation from the old year into the new) as is when the moon is in Libra (the sign represented by scales).

※ Add aromatics that elementally balance each other such as frankincense and myrrh, pine-apple and pear, or rosemary and spearmint (all of which are categorized as "Fire" and "Water," respectively). Note: It is possible to try to balance all four Elements but the aroma produced isn't always pleasant. Some Air aromatics include almond, lavender, and mulberry. Earth aromatics include honeysuckle, patchouli, and vetivert.

※ Use oppositely colored candles (black and white being ideal). Alternatively, purple is considered a color that promotes harmony.

※ Include other components like fluorite (which promotes balance), a yin yang symbol carved into the candle, or a feather as a portable charm (against which souls were balanced in ancient Egyptian mythology).

Spells

Perform this spell at midnight or noon. If you're dealing with balance in intuitive/emotional matters, midnight is better; if you're dealing with conscious/logical/mundane matters, noon is better. You'll need a black candle, a white candle, one candle that represents self, and a bathroom scale. Put the scale on a flat surface where it can remain undisturbed for three days. Put the candles in secure holders on top of the scale. Make sure they're equally separated and form an upward pointing triangle (a very stable geometric design).

Begin by carving a symbol into the candle that represents the part of your life to which you wish to bring balance. Light the black and the white candle at noon or midnight on day one saying:

"Symmetry enhance, restore the balance!"

Let the candles burn for three hours (to encourage balance in body, mind, and spirit). On day two, repeat the process but say the incantation *twice* and move the black and white candle closer toward the one that represents you. On day three, repeat the process again, but this time say the incantation *three* times, then light the candle of self with the other two (blow these out and set them aside). Spend as much of the next three hours as possible in prayer and meditation using the remaining candlelight as your focus. Keep a bit of the wax as a portable charm to encourage ongoing balance. Note: Every time you weigh yourself in the future, you can repeat the incantation to keep the magick moving!

⚭ ⌒❡ ❞⌒⚬

For this spell you'll need 2 cups of candle wax (remnants from other candle burning spells is fine as long as the energies there correlate with your goal), one-fourth teaspoon each of frankincense and myrrh powder, a piece of wick, a two and one-half cup heat-safe container (oiled), and a fluorite crystal (small). Gently melt the wax over a low flame (use a non-aluminum pan if possible). Stir counterclockwise to banish chaos, focusing on your goal while saying:

"Turn and change, turn and change,
Magick is to turn and change."

Once the wax is completely melted, sprinkle in the frankincense and myrrh saying:

"As this candle burns, balance returns."

Let the candle wax cool a bit. While it does, place the fluorite crystal in the bottom of the container you've chosen and suspend the wick by tying it to a pencil or knife placed across the top of the container. Slowly pour the wax into the mold (this helps deter air bubbles). Cool completely, then remove the container by dipping the whole thing into hot water briefly. Burn whenever you wish to reestablish equilibrium. Add energy to the candle by repeating the original incantation when you light it.

Banishing

When negative energy, bad luck, or malintent surround, it's time for a good old-fashioned banishing spell. I do issue caution on how you devise yours, however. I know of one person who tried to banish the negativity from the office and ended up inadvertently banishing the people who carried that negativity! This is a good example as to why specificity is important in spellcraft.

* Time your spells for the waning or dark moon, or for the noon hour, to shine a light on the darkness that surrounds.
* Add aromatics such as pine, rosemary, and woodruff.
* Use black or brown candles (to ground out the negativity).
* Include other components such as beans (once used to turn away the evil eye), a cross or star (protective symbols), and salt (an all-purpose banishing component).

Spells

Into a black or brown candle carve a symbol of the area of your life in which the difficulty exists. Be thoughtful and purposeful as you carve, knowing that your intention is to simply banish the negative energies or influences there without harm to anyone else. Light this candle come the dark moon saying:

"Candle burn, burn, burn; negativity turn, turn, turn;
Good luck return, return, return."

Leave this candle to burn out of it's own accord (in a fire safe container) then dispose of the wax so that you literally put the negativity away from yourself.

For this spell, you'll need to find a black candle that has been *dipped* that color (meaning the inside is white and there's only a layer of black outside). Leave the top half black, but gently scrape away the bottom half so it reveals the white underneath. On the bottom part of the candle, carve symbols of your hopes and wishes, then dab them with a bit of personal perfume or cologne. Leave the top half *blank*. Place a straight pin in the center (this marks the turn-around point). Light the candle saying:

"Negativity ends as the magick pin bends.
Negativity destroy, I reclaim joy;
As the candle burns, by and by, all energies are purified."

Turn away from the candle and do not return until it has completely burned out.

By the way, a neat visual alternative on this spell is to let the candle burn down to the pin then turn it over in its stand. This "puts out" the negative energy and allows you to "light" (put into motion) the positive energy, giving more support to the represented hopes and wishes.

Collect one black candle and one candle whose color represents the area of your life in which the trouble lies. If in a relationship, for example, use red or pink. Place these two candles adjacent to each other on a flat surface. Light the candles every night for seven nights at dusk (the time of ending/closure) saying:

> *"Negativity return from whence you came,*
> *my life will n'er be the same!*
> *Happiness and success I now reclaim."*

Each night you do this, move the black candle further and further away from the other one (slowly moving it closer to a door in your home). On the morning of the eighth day, take the remnants of the black candle outside and let it melt in the sun, banishing that darkness with light. Dispose of properly. Keep the other candle wrapped in a white cloth (symbolic of protection). You can reuse it for similar purposes.

Beginnings

If you're about to start a new job, move to a new home, begin a new project, or enter into a partnership and would like to get things off on the right foot, these spells are a great companion to the mundane planning and preparations you're making:

❋ Time your spells for dawn, the season of Spring, or when the moon is just starting to wax.

❋ Add aromatics such as lemon and peach (for the longevity of the project), heather and rose (luck), and ginger (success).

❋ Use white candles or ones whose color represents the area of your life in which the genesis is happening (such as red for a marriage, green for a job, etc.).

❈ Include other components such as seedlings,
a buzzer (to denote the beginning), flower
buds, etc.

Spells

On the morning when everything is going into place
for your new start, take a white candle and dress it with a
bit of lemon juice or oil. Hold the candle in both hands
visualizing the very best outcomes possible from your
endeavor. Pour all that excitement and positive energy into
the wax while saying:

"A bright beginning let it be, let it be.
A light in the darkness, let me see, let me see!
All that was and shall be...open the windows of insight
to me."

Next, hold the candle in one hand and light it with the
other. Let a few drops of wax fall on a piece of paper at
least 6 inches below the flame. Continue focusing on your
endeavor. Put the candle in a holder and continue letting
it burn for blessings while you look at the pattern made by
the wax. You can interpret these patterns similarly to those
made by inkblots or tea leaves. Here are some sample interpretive values:

❈ A circular blob is a very good omen for
unity and completing a cycle.

❈ A squarish blob implies good financial
outcomes and good foundations.

❈ A lot of separate drops indicate you may be
scattering your energy in too many directions
or diverse options presenting themselves.

❈ A heart shape indicates this is a labor of
love, or that you will receive help and
support from a loved one.

❈ A smooth river (or s-shape) of wax
    indicates a likewise smooth, flowing
    transition.

For this spell, you'll need the left over candle wax from
the first activity here and a seed or very small seedling.
Choose the seed so that it symbolizes your endeavor. For
example, for a new monetary investment, you might choose
an alfalfa sprout, whereas for the beginning of a new friendship, you might choose a lemon seed.

Melt the wax (a couple of tablespoons is more than
enough). Let this wax cool so that you can easily wrap it
around a seed or seedling. As you mold the wax gently
around the seed think of it like a new "baby" to whom
you're giving as much love and attention as possible. As
you add more layers of wax so the seed is fully protected,
consider using an incantation such as:

*"Wrapped in safety, by magickal arts, Goddess bless this
work of my heart.
Wrapped in love and a waxen ring, Goddess grant me a
great beginning!*

Take this charm with you when you venture out on
your new quest!

Birthdays

*"You know you're getting old when the candles cost
more than the cake."*

—Bob Hope

A friend of mine used to tell me that on your birthday
you're the most important person in the world. That day
is certainly worth a moment's pause to celebrate and do a

spell or two to help you integrate the last year and bless the coming one. And don't forget to blow out the candles on your birthday cake with a wish. In Greece, this tradition began with the followers of Artemis who made moon shaped, candle-decorated cakes on her traditional festival day. When the candles went out, they released the wishes to the goddess herself.

* Time your spells for the morning so they set the tone for the entire day.

* Add aromatics such as hyacinth, lavender, and lily of the valley (all of which encourage happiness).

* Use your favorite color candle, an astrologically aligned candle *(see Appendix B)*, or birthday candles (of course!).

* Include other components such as your favorite cake, decorations, a party horn, upbeat music, or anything else with a celebratory and upbeat feeling to it.

Spells

For this spell you'll need twelve candles placed in a circle so they're spaced out like the face of a clock. Dab each with a bit of your favorite cologne or perfume. Beginning at the candle in the one o'clock position, light the candles clockwise in the Circle saying:

One month of blessings;
"One month of health;
One month of joy;
One month of wealth;
One month at home;
One month to away;
One month of laughter;

One month to play;
One month of solitude;
One month of Peace.
A whole year of magick, may it never cease!"

Bear in mind that you can change the last word of each wish to better suit your circumstances. I've just often found it's easier to remember rhymed incantations. Leave the candles to burn for one minute for every year you've been alive, then keep them for the following year. When the candles finally start getting too small to use, light fresh tapers from them the following year and remelt the wax to use for something special.

On a side note, you can perform this ritual every year for a child, then give them the candles you've kept when they come of age.

This is an adaptation of the traditional birthday wish. Take the candles you intend to use on your cake and rub some lavender oil into them (for peace and joy) while saying:

"Flower of blue...flower with a calming hue,
bring me joy, bring me peace,
good health and blessings ner' cease."

Remember to focus on your wish while blowing out all the candles on your cake!

Blessing

Who couldn't use a few more blessings on a regular basis (or minimally a greater awareness and appreciation of those we already have)? These spells are designed to attract divine good fortune, so if you can call upon a personal god or goddess to assist in these, all the better.

❋ Time your spells for special occasions (such as your birthday or the birth of a child), when the moon is full, when the moon is in Pisces or Taurus, or noon (the sun is a traditional symbol of blessing).

❄ Add aromatics such as elder flowers (actually most blossoming plants will work).

❄ Use warm colored candles (gold, yellow) or white (the color of Spirit).

❄ Include other components such as barley, corn, mint, heather, water, bread, or carnelian (all of which have associations with divine favor).

Spells:

This is a very simple blessing spell specifically for your magickal candles. Lay out your candles on a surface (your altar is a good choice). Now, place your hands palm down on top of them. The hand is an ancient conduit for blessing seen in many global spiritual traditions. Visualize a bright light from overhead flowing downward through your arms into the candles. Whisper a prayer to whatever vision of the God/dess you wish, asking for His/Her blessings on these tools. If you wish, you can make the prayer specific so that it designates the use for each candle (such as one for peace, one for Money Magick, etc.). Continue until you feel the palms of your hands growing slightly warm, then wrap the candles in a soft white cloth (also good for polishing), storing them safely away until needed.

Rituals of self-blessing are very popular among Witches. Because each person strives to be their own guru/guide/priest/priestess, it's natural to perform such functions for oneself. Additionally, we believe that in order to truly help others, we must first be whole in body, mind, and spirit. This means that regular blessings become a maintenance method with the goal of wholeness and ongoing rapport with Spirit in mind.

For this mini-ritual any candle will do, but white is a good choice. Carve images of the types of blessings you wish to bring into your life along the length of the candle (preferably in the same order from top to bottom, as you're going to request them from the God/dess). Light the candle and concentrate on the first symbol. As it begins to melt, speak your prayer. For example, if the first symbol was a heart your prayer might be:

"God/dess bless my heart that I might be open to giving and receiving love."

Continue this way until all the symbols have melted. Put out the candle and light it the next time you need a few blessings to manifest quickly.

Cleansing (Purification)

Ongoing spiritual house cleaning is very important to magickal practitioners. I can't tell you the number of times someone has unwittingly dumped negative or off-center vibes on my proverbial doorstep. While I don't mind "sharing," this is something I can easily do without! Additionally, people living high-stress lives or in crowded areas often suffer from psychic and spiritual clutter similar to what I just described, even without someone having visited. Cleansing and purification spells can help offset the nasty results that can happen when this clutter is allowed to build up.

* Time your spells for early Spring (spring cleaning), when the moon is in Aries, during the waning moon, or for when you're doing your regular house cleaning.
* Add purgative aromatics such as pine, lemon, clove, frankincense and myrrh, or sandalwood.
* Use black candles to banish negativity or white for purity. Blue for reestablishing peace is also an option.

❋ Include other components such as amber (which traps unwanted energies), onyx (or other black stones), salt (a natural cleanser), and any of your traditional cleaning tools (a broom).

First gather together eight white candles and one black one. Set these into very secure holders placed into the pattern of an eight-pointed star on the floor in which you can sit comfortably to meditate. Keep the black candle in the middle with you. If you don't get dripless candles make sure any floor or carpeting is protected from the resulting wax drippings before you begin.

Light the black candle first and focus your attention wholly on it. Breathe deeply and evenly. Concentrate on releasing any darkness or negativity into that candle (see this as brackish goo that saturates into that candles blackness). When you feel empty, blow out the black candle and turn it upside down in its holder.

Next, light all the white candles that surround you (move as needed so they're within a comfortable reach). As you light each one, say:

"Away all negativity and bane,
Only pure light-energy remain."

Now sit in the center of the circle of light you've created. You are now the candle—the wick of your spirit being reenergized and empowered by the purity around you. Stay as long as you wish in this clean space, letting it sparkle throughout your aura. Carry that freshness with you.

Note: the candles from this activity may be reused for similar ends if enough remains.

❧ ⟨⟨ ✦ ⟩⟩ ❧

Pick out a candle to represent yourself. If possible, decorate the candle in some manner to further personalize it. I recommend repeating this spell over three progressive nights of the waxing to dark moon (to banish bad vibes). As you light your candle each night repeat this incantation three times:

"_____is my name.

Like the burning of the flame, Purity I claim
First in body; Next in mind,
With this light all darkness bind.
Then in spirit and in soul
I'm now cleansed, refreshed, and whole."

You can keep and reuse the candle for any purity, cleansing, or similar spells.

Communication

To speak or write and to be not only heard but understood is the foundation to good relationships, effective business management, and many other things in life. Unfortunately, there are many times in our discourse when we feel like those involved are speaking two (if not more) different languages and there isn't a translator in sight! Communication spells and rituals can help bridge the gap between what's said and what's actually meant.

* Time your spells for when the moon is in Aries. Fridays and Wednesdays also support this energy. Additionally, consider the theme of the matter at hand as a clue to good timing for your magick. If you're speaking about love, you might want to cast your spell during the full moon, for example.

* Add Air-oriented aromatics (the Element of communication) such as almond, bergamot, lavender, and pine.

* Use yellow colored candles (attuned to the Air Element and effective expression).

❄ Include other components such as yellow paper and ink, a telephone cord, and stones such
   as beryl, carnelian, and hematite (all of which
   improve your ability to be understood clearly).

Gather together a sheet of yellow paper and a yellow
candle. On the paper, write a description of the person
with whom (or situation in which) you'd like to communicate more effectively. Fold the paper in half on itself, then
in half again, and in half again (three times all told), repeating this incantation each time you fold it:

"Uncertainty and miscommunication, be gone for good.
By this spell, let my words be understood!"

Now take the candle in hand and tip it so that a few
drops of yellow wax affix the edges of the paper (like a letter seal). Add another incantation to this process, such as:

"Ideas and words, no longer wait,
Help me to communicate!
Truth be keen, never bend, so other people comprehend."

Carry this paper with you into any situation where you
feel your ideas or words might be misunderstood. Note, however, that once the core issues have been resolved, you should
burn or bury the paper. This is really a "one shot" spell.

⸙ ⸙ ⸙

This spell uses candied almonds and a yellow candle as
components, and is particularly helpful for clearing up mis-
communications in a relationship. Wait to cast the spell
until Friday, which got its name from the Goddess Frigg
who protected marriages. Place the candle and the candies
on your altar or another area where you typically work spells.
Light the candle, saying:

"The light of good intention shines,
its energy saturating the sweet

*treats so that my words might likewise
be sweet and well received."*

Visualize the light of the candle saturating every bit of the almonds. Leave the candle to burn itself out (if it's safe to do so) then store the candies in a portable, airtight container. Enjoy one just before going into a difficult discussion with a loved one.

Conscious Mind

Come hither, and I shall light a candle of understanding in thine heart, which shall not be put out.

—Apocrypha. 2 Esdras, 14:25.

Some people might wonder what the logical, rational mind has to do with spirituality and magick. My answer to that question is everything! Our conscious mind helps us to know what we need, when we need it, and provides ideas as to how to fulfill those needs both magickally and mundanely. Spells that support the conscious mind also help with overall alertness, our ability to enumerate, and knowledge-oriented skills.

⁂ Time your spells for the noon hour (or when it's sunny) as the sun stresses the logical/rational self. When the moon is in Leo is a good alternative because of the strong solar nature of this sign.

⁂ Add aromatics such as rosemary, which is said to improve memory. Lilac and honeysuckle are alternatives that support mental keenness.

⁂ Use red, yellow, orange, or gold colored candles (a nice blend of Air and Fire).

⁂ Include other components such as fluorite, aventurine, sphene, maze patterns, and walnuts, all of which accent cognitive functions.

For this spell, you'll need nothing more than a candle (your choice of color) and a toothpick. On a morning when you know you're going to need to be particularly "on" mentally, get up a little early. Sit in the light of the morning sun and carve an emblem of the area of your life where mental accuracy is most needed/required. Focus wholly on your goal, then place the candle into a holder and light it, saying:

> *"Logic's power takes hold—uncertainty bind,*
> *with confidence and alertness,*
> *empower my conscious mind."*

Repeat this incantation several times, allowing your voice to grow naturally. When you feel yourself completely filled with confidence and warm solar energy, blow out the candle and seize the day!

☙ ⌘ ❧

If you'd like a portable charm that supports the conscious mind, begin by saving the candle from the first spell under this topic. You'll also need a 3"x 3" swatch of yellow fabric, a piece of yarn about 6 inches long, a fluorite crystal and some rosemary. Light the candle, repeating the incantation provided above. Visualize the light of the candle saturating the cloth, crystal and herb. Now, place the fluorite crystal in the middle of the cloth saying:

> *"This represents the successful application of my skills*
> *and knowledge."*

Sprinkle the rosemary over the stone saying:

> *"This represents information that stays with me."*

Drip some of the candle wax into the bundle, then tie it together like a sachet saying:

> *"A keen wit and a keen mind, herein I bind."*

Carry this with you or keep it where its energies will do the most good (like an office desk drawer). If you ever need speedy help from your conscious self, open the sachet and cast one piece of rosemary to the winds with your wish.

Decisions (uncertainty)

Every day we're faced with decisions ranging from what route to take to work, to determining the right career path! Very few of those choices boil down to a simple yes or no. In fact, many of the decisions with which we're faced have numerous options to measure. It's not surprising then that we sometimes find it difficult to sit back and sort it all out. When you're having trouble with a decision try a spell, ritual, or perhaps a divination method to help you finalize things.

❋ Time your spells similarly to those for the conscious mind, as decisions rely heavily on the logical, rational self. Alternative timings include when the moon is in Sagittarius or Libra, when the moon is full (for really keen instincts), and on Tuesday (for good strategy).

❋ Add aromatics such as vanilla, rosemary, nutmeg, and apple, all of which encourage alertness and improved observation skills.

❋ Use black and white colored candles (especially for binary or yes/no type questions).

❋ Include other components such as a coin, straw, a hat, or anything else people typically use when making random choices.

Begin with a piece of white paper, one black candle, and one white candle. Dab both candles with an aromatic you prefer. If you're not using the suggested ones, consider finding a scent that mirrors the theme of your choice. For example, if choosing between lovers, try rose. Light the candle side-by-side saying:

> "A *light in the dark,*
> *insight abide—between the options,*
> *help me decide!"*

Carefully take both candles in one hand (your strong hand) and tip them so they drip on the paper. Keep concentrating on your dilemma for about two minutes.

Return the candles to their holder. If the black one has melted more than the white, then the course of action you preferred is not the best one. You can gain additional insight by scrying the wax drippings using this brief list as a starting point for interpretive values:

- ❊ Black wax covering the white wax: This indicates while your ideas were sound, the results will be negative if you continue on this course.

- ❊ White wax covering the black wax: This indicates a rough start, but good finish! Stick with the present plan.

- ❊ Lots of intermingled black and white dots: This indicates a very uncertain future. The web of fate is tangled right now. You may want to wait a while before making a choice and gather more information.

- ❊ Dots scattered all over the paper: This indicates trying to do too much; scattering your energy to the winds. You need to narrow your focus and the choices at hand to something more manageable.

By the way, you can use the resulting piece of paper as part of a portable decision-making charm, too. Just wrap it around a coin and keep it handy for when you're pressed for a decision.

A second method of divination requires two black candles, two white candles, and a pendulum of some kind. You can make a pendulum yourself out of a length of string (three times the length of your hand to your elbow is good). To this string tie anything that has a discernable point so you can determine the direction of movement. Place the white candles at North and South of a circular area on a tabletop. Place the black candles West and East and light all four.

Next put the elbow of your strong hand carefully on the table outside the circle created by the candles. Hold the pendulum string so it sets a few inches above the table surface in the middle of the candles. Make sure it's still, then concentrate on ONE of the potential paths ahead of you. If the pendulum begins to move between the two white candles (up and down) that's an affirmative answer, whereas between the black candles (left to right) is negative. Bear in mind, if you're asking several questions, you can have *more than one* positive answer in this method, meaning those two options are the best possible ones to ponder, and perhaps use those as the focal point for a fresh divinatory attempt.

Death

Most Neo-Pagans see death not just as an ending but a beginning. Nonetheless, the loss of someone in our lives touches the heart and soul of what it means to be human. Typically, candles participate in what Wiccans call a Summerland ritual (to honor a soul's passing and help it along toward its next existence) or in a memorial ritual that commemorates a deceased spirit's birth or death date as a celebration of how much that person meant to us.

❋ Time your spells for dusk (to symbolize an ending) or for dawn (to represent renewal). Alternatively use the anniversary date of birth or death.

✳ Add aromatics such as cypress, frankincense and myrrh (traditional funerary aromatics), or a perfume/cologne/scent preferred by the person being commemorated.

✳ Use white candles to symbolize the eternal soul and Spirit.

✳ Include other components that are meaningful to you and the participants in the ritual.

Set up an altar (any flat surface) with a candle to represent the individual, a picture of the person you're honoring and other items that remind you of him or her (such as if they smoked a pipe, have pipe tobacco). As each person joining you for this mini-ritual to bring a white candle and a personal message to share with the group or the spirit of the person whose passed over. You need not create sacred space for this ritual unless you wish to do so.

When everyone has gathered, put the individual's candle on the altar and light it saying:

"_____(insert name of person) hail and welcome.
We reach to you with our hearts—our minds—our spirits.
We reach beyond the veil. Bend down close and listen.
This is your moment.
Let your spirit soar as it hears our words and wishes."

Next, each person in turn lights their candle from the first, and speaks whatever is in his or her heart. Feel free to laugh, cry, and generally support each other. Relax and talk in the light of the candles for as long as you wish.

When it comes time to depart, have everyone join hands. Direct your words once more to the individual's candle:

"Thank you for joining us...and hearing our heartfelt words. Know you are missed, but that we celebrate the liberation of your spirit. We pray for your speedy return to Oneness and Unity with the god/dess and hold you forever in our hearts."

All say:

"*HAIL AND FAREWELL!*"

Blow out the candles.

When someone is suffering from a terminal illness, and you know their time is short, you can make them a special candle to burn when they feel the need for strength and comfort. For this I suggest a pale blue candle (the color of peace) into which you focus all your will and prayers toward a calm and dignified transition every night at dusk. For example, when my friend was ailing, I prayed with my palms facing downward over the candle that she would not see herself as her disease, but as the beautiful person she was. Similarly, I chanted for things like painlessness and fulfillment. I then gave that candle to her and her family to light as they needed (and later to use as part of her Summerland ritual).

I use this personal example rather than give exacting details because rituals and other spiritual workings for death, like birth and marriage, are *very* personal. They need to come from your heart.

Divination

Divination by candles is called Lychnomancy. In Ireland, people chose the color of the candle they used for such divinations by the question's topic (such as red for love, and green for money).

❋ Time your spells for midnight or during the waxing or full moon. Midnight is called the Witching Hour and the full moon emphasizes psychic abilities. Alternatively, you can consider New Year's, Beltane, Lammas, and Hallows, all of which are thought to be very good times for divinatory efforts.

❄ Add aromatics such as cinnamon, clover, honeysuckle, fennel, and nutmeg (all of which aid psychic insight).

❄ Use yellow candles to represent the Air Element or follow the Irish tradition and choose your color according to the question at hand.

❄ Include other components that also support divinatory efforts such as marigold petals, beans, amethyst and silver.

To divine by the candle's flame, put the tape holder on a flat surface where you can sit nearby (about two feet away from you). Think of a question that's been nagging at you and focus on the candle's flame. Allow everything else in the room to fade from view. Here is a list of interpretive values for what you may see:

❄ A halo around the flame indicates trouble of some sort looming on the horizon.

❄ A dim burning candle is a negative omen. If you were making any plans, slow down or hold off.

❄ A candle that dances rather vigorously implies sudden changes.

❄ A brightly burning, steady candle is a very good omen and luck.

❄ A sparking candle portends important news forthcoming about the question at hand.

❄ A candle that smothers and goes out quickly is a *very* bad sign.

❄ A divided flame shows loyalties or interests likewise divided.

❄ A blue flame indicates the presence of spirits or guides.

❄ Circles or rings around the flame indicate joy and fulfillment.

Some people find that putting the candle in front of a mirror and focusing on the flame in the mirror, or looking at the flame through the facets of a crystal yields more success (note choose the crystal according to the question or use a clear faceted quartz). Also, should you have floating candles in the house, you can use these as well. Put them in the water, lighting them clockwise, then observe all the flames as they move and mingle.

వ ($\sim$ ᵛ᷎ᵗ᷉

A third alternative is using candle wax rather than scrying the flame. In this case, you use one or several colors of candles and think of your question while the candle wax drips into a bowl of water. Observe the patterns that form on the surface both while the wax is cooling and then afterward when it hardens. You'll find you can often get several different impressions this way (akin to looking for pictures in clouds or inkblots).

If you'd like to use one of your scrying candles as part of a spell to improve other types of divination efforts (tarot, runes, etc.), by all means, do so! Carve the image of an eye into the candle and then dress the candle in a psychically enhancing aromatic saying:

"The light of insight burns, the Site returns. The truth reveal; nothing conceal."

Light the candle just before beginning your reading.

I highly recommend you take notes of your divinatory efforts and what comes out of them. It will help you mark your progress and also assist in figuring out what processes work best for you.

Dreams

What's in a dream? Well if you asked our ancestors, the answer would have been quite a lot! We find written documents dating to 1350 B.C.E. in Babylon that speak of various symbols in our dreamscape. Egyptians had dream oracles. Hittite prayers ask for the gods to reveal themselves in dreams, and they even had a special god who presided over the dream world—Ziqiqu. Hebrews trusted in dreams to indicate the will of YHWH, and Native Americans look to dreams and visionary states as a means of speaking to the spirit world.

Some of the world's most notable minds respected the art of dream divination. Socrates rewrote *Aesop's Fables* because he believed that one of his dreams instructed this course of action. Hippocrates (the father of medicine) felt that dreams could reveal the source of illness or alternatively symbolize a previously unknown physical problem. Other dream advocates include Julius Caesar, St. John, Mozart, and Benjamin Franklin. And what of Neo-Pagans? We feel that dreams can be far more than just an elaborate subconscious filing system. Rather, we see them as a way for spirit guides, and even the gods themselves, to speak to us. With this in mind, how can we use Candle Magick to help that communicative process along? Here are some examples:

* Time your spells for any night, but best when the moon is waxing to full. Monday (the moon's day), or the moon in Capricorn (discovering things from one's higher self).

* Add aromatics such as sage, rose, thyme, and rosemary (so you remember the dreams when they come).

* Use blue or purple candles (a dreamy color) or yellow candles, which are associated with spiritual missives.

* Include other components that are tied to dreaming such as agate, amethyst, coral, silver, grapes, wine, beer, and dream catchers.

Choose a night when you know you have plenty of time for rest. Take a dark blue candle into your sleep space with some incense. Light both the candle and the incense and sit comfortably focusing on the flame of the candle. Repeat this incantation three times:

"As I will it, so shall it be.
On the wings of the wind—a dream.
On the flames of truth—a dream.
On the waves of understanding—a dream.
On the soil of fertility—a dream.
Come to me! Reveal to me! So mote it be!"

Look at the candle for a few seconds longer so that you can see its image clearly in your mind's eye, then blow it out. Lie down, visualize the candle, and whisper your incantation to yourself as you drift off to sleep. Make notes immediately upon rising of any visions that come to you (tape recording the memories also works).

Bear in mind that for those who have trouble remembering their dreams, it may take a little time and effort to be successful. If you find yourself in this category, I'd suggest trying a relaxing, candlelit bath before bed. Add some lavender, rose, and/or geranium essence to the water. If you sprinkle a bit of fine glitter into bubbles, all the better. It creates a very dreamy atmosphere. Just please be sure to take yourself into bed when you start feeling sleepy for obvious safety reasons.

This spell is intended both to bring a significant dream and help you remember it. Begin with a blue candle dabbed with rose and lavender oil. Carve an eye into it (this need not be a great artistic work—just recognizable). Hold an amethyst crystal in your weak hand while you light the candle with your strong hand. Repeat this incantation slowly eight times while allowing yourself to relax and get sleepy.

"Dreaming right
Dreaming true
Keep my visions clear
When the sun breaks through!"

Blow out the candle, put the amethyst under your pillow, and lie down. Whisper the incantation to yourself until you fall asleep. Make notes immediately upon waking of any visions that come.

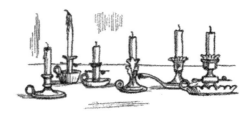

Employment

"My candle burns at both ends; it will not last the night.
But ah, my foes, and oh,
my friends—it gives a lovely light"

—Edna St. Vincent Millay

For many people (if not most), employment is a part of the happiness equation. Having a sense of purpose, taking pride in a job well done, and supporting one's self or family all tenure a sense of mundane actualization. So it's not surprising to discover unemployed, under-employed, or unappreciated employees suffering from depression and other stress-related disorders. The purposes behind employment spells, meditations, and rituals are to either improve the situation you're in, or create new (and more fulfilling) opportunities.

❊ Time your spells for the waxing to full moon (manifestation), when the moon is in Virgo, or any time in the late Spring/early Summer when the Earth thrives with bounty.

❊ Add aromatics such as ginger, clove, almond, and orange all of which support prosperity and security.

❊ Use green or gold candles for money, or other colors that correlate directly to your trade (for example a botanist might use dark green or brown to illustrate the Earth Element, whereas a nurse might use shoot green candles to stress health).

❊ Include other potential components and symbols that represent your work and your goals within that position. For example, if you're hoping to move into management, a tie or business clothing might be part of your overall ritual. Business cards are also excellent components, especially after interviews.

Spells

You will need a candle (your choice of color) and either a personal business card, or those from supervisors or recent interviews. The cards from supervisors are for when you're working Advancement Magick. Those from recent interviews are for opening the right doors.

Prop the business card up so it's easily seen in front of the candleholder. Starting just after the first signs of a newly waxing moon, every morning at dawn (the time of hope), light the candle and speak a prayer to your vision of Deity. Be very specific in your goals, hopes, and dreams. If time allows, also stop for a moment and visualize those details clearly. Continue this procedure every day until something changes or the candle wax expires. If manifestation hasn't occurred yet, carry a bit of the remaining drippings, adhered to the business cards as a portable charm that keeps the energy moving forward.

＆ ＇＆ ＊＇＆

For this spell, you'll need a small symbol of your trade. A secretary might use a pen, a carpenter, a screw, and so forth. Light a green candle and have the emblem at hand. You'll want to add an incantation, repeated four times (the number of Earth- and career-oriented energy) that illustrates your goal. For example, if you're up for a raise or promotion you might say:

> *"My talents and dedication like this candle shine!*
> *That raise or promotion will soon be mine!"*

Or if you're trying to land a new job:

*"Have no worries, there's naught to fear.
I'll soon begin a new career!"*

After repeating the incantation dab a bit of the candle wax on the symbol of your choosing and carry it with you until your goal manifests. Afterward keep it in a safe place to, likewise, protect your new position.

Energy (Power)

When people joke with me about broom-wielding Witches, I often say that I prefer a vacuum cleaner (as in the now famous words of a popular television series, Home Improvement—*More power!*). Seriously, having steady physical, emotional, and spiritual energy isn't only important to comedic moments and magick, but also to your health. With so many folks multi-tasking and wearing many hats, however, there are many times when we do, indeed, need *more power*! That's exactly where these spells come in.

❋ Time your spells for when the sun is bright in the sky (Fire) or when the moon is full (for the fullness of Water-oriented energies). Thursday's (Thor's day), and throughout the seasons of Spring and Summer.

❋ Add zealous aromatics such as cinnamon, ginger, carnation, rosemary, and vanilla

❋ Use red- (the color of life's blood) or orange-colored candles.

❋ Include other potential components and symbols that represent increase (such as an upward pointing candle, a "greater than" mathematical icon, and the rising tide of a lake or ocean).

When possible, I like to perform this spell when the tide is coming in on a beach. If logistics don't allow this setting, you can use a slowly rising tub or sink of water as an alternative. Carve a symbol on your chosen candle that represents the area of your life requiring more energy or power. Place that candle in the sand near the water's edge, but not so close that it will get washed out to sea. If you're using a tub or sink, put it in a self-contained candleholder in the middle of the slowly rising water.

Now light the candle and sit nearby, focusing on its flame. Use this simple incantation:

"Energy arise in me!"

Start out whispering, then let your voice slowly grow louder and louder as the water rises. When you feel the same swell within yourself, stand up and open your arms to the sky to receive the energy. If you've gone to the beach, blow out the candle and carefully reclaim it. At home, you can allow the water to douse the candle, but do take care that no wax goes down the drain (or you'll end up using all that newly claimed energy to fix the pipes!). In either situation, the candle can be used in another similar spell or brought to the altar of a ritual where you'd like some extra power available to support the working.

For this spell you'll need a candle and a 3-foot length of rope, yarn, or heavy cord. Wait until noon, preferably on a sunny day, and take both outside to a table. Put the candle in the middle of the table with the rope around its base so that you can grab both ends easily for tying during the spell. Light the candle, saying:

*"As the sun rises high in the sky,
as the flame on this candle grows full in this magick hour,
so too POWER!"*

Next, grasp the two ends of the rope (one with each hand). You're going to knot this rope three times saying:

*"Power within and bound,
release when called upon and unwound!"*

Leave this in the sunlight until the candle burns itself out or the wax begins to melt from the heat. Dab a bit of the melted wax on each knot. Keep this someplace safe, only undoing *one* knot when a need arises. **Never**, however, unbind the last knot (this is an old custom). When you've used two, you should re-work the spell and replace the knots that have been used.

Enact this spell on Summer Solstice. Come the first rays of dawn, light a golden-colored candle saying:

*"Welcome the sun!
As your light shines fully on this day,
So too does energy shine throughout my body, mind,
and spirit."*

Next using the flame of the candle, light a stick of ginger incense, saying:

*"I share the candle's flame with this incense,
so it may share its energy with me."*

Sit in the light of the sun, absorbing its power and breathing deeply until you feel fully recharged.

Fear

Among the many emotions common to humans, fear is one of the most debilitating. Anyone who has ever experienced a panic attack can verify how fear (no matter how real or imagined the source) can stop a person cold. In the process of learning to become our own Priests or Preistesses, we also have to become a good self-counselor for those times when any emotion threatens to capsize our life's mental, physical, or spiritual forward-moving boat. One of the solutions I've found most helpful is just doing something positive! The minute we believe we can change our reality—we can! So, why not blend a little Candle Magick into the mix as part of that positive action?

* Time your spells for the waning to dark moon, when the sun is shining (to banish the shadows), during the month of October (for protection), or when the moon is in Gemini.

* Add aromatics such as borage or yarrow, both known for their courage-producing qualities.

* Use black candles (for banishing) or dark blue to encourage tranquility.

* Include other potential components and symbols such as amethyst and tea, both of which provide calm focus. Alternatively, eye agate, salt, and turquoise provide protective energies.

For this spell I recommend a black candle, specifically one large enough to burn for about one hour a day over nine days, and one white candle (any size). At dusk each night, for eight nights, focus all your fears and uncertainties into the wax (it sometimes helps to actually hold the candle in your hands while doing this part of the process). Then, light the candle, saying:

"Let my confidence burn as surely as the flame.
Let fears melt into the shadows, banished by light and
courage.
Let doubt be conquered by will and resolve.
Strength and surety are all about...
I know no fear...I know no doubt.
So mote it be."

The morning after the eighth night, rise at dawn. Pick up the black candle and break it apart (this symbolizes breaking fear's hold over you). Replace it in the candleholder with the white candle. Light it saying:

"It is done, the battle is won;
All fears are tamed; courage I claim."

Let this candle burn out naturally.

Gather together a small strip of paper, pen, string or thread, candle, toothpick, and some salt. Write the word "fear" on the paper. Next, near the middle of the candle etch the word "courage" using the toothpick (the word should wrap around the circumference of the candle). Tie the snippet of paper to the candle over the word you've just carved.

Last, but not least, light the candle. Direct all your fears and misgivings into that small piece of paper. Watch as the candle of courage literally burns it away. Take the resulting ashes and release them to the Four Winds with thankfulness for your new outlooks.

For this spell, you'll need a tub or shower, lavender and pine blended bath salts, and blue candles (for re-establishing

peace). Place the candle in a safe location near the tub
and sprinkle a little of the bath salts around it saying:

> *"Surrounded with courage, safe and secure, peace rise
> within, my spirit assure!"*

Now, get in the tub or shower (Note: If you're taking a
shower you can use a piece of gauze to hold the salts. Hang
this off the showerhead so they're slowly released onto your
body). Visualize all the negativity associated with fear being
totally purified and washed down the drain by the salts. Keep
some of the salt that you placed around the candle as a
portable charm to keep bravery close by (release a pinch of
this to a South wind when you need backbone quickly).

Fertility

As with the misunderstanding that occurs regarding
the applications for the word "abundance" in a magickal
sense, sometimes people only associate Fertility Magick
with getting pregnant. This need not be so. Our ancestors
often worked Fertility Magick for their animals and for
the earth, and you can too! The reverse also holds true.
By working fertility spells a little differently you can spiritually help avoid conception (this might be good for animals who have not been spayed yet, or people for whom
some forms of contraception are not healthy). Note: Under NO circumstances should spiritual efforts become a
substitute for mundane protections. Remember, in magick
and life, common sense goes a long way!

* Time your spells for dawn, Spring, a full moon,
  a Monday or when the moon is in Pisces. April
  is a good month for Fertility Magick.
* Add aromatics such as musk, vervain,
  geranium, hawthorn petals, and pine.
* Use shoot green or yellow candles.

❄ Include other potential components and symbols that represent your goals. Newly blossoming plants, seeds, eggs, and nuts are four choices. Other components traditionally associated with fertility include coral and agate stones.

You'll need an egg, some seeds, and a candle of your choice for this spell. Choose the seeds so that they represent the area of your life to which you wish to bring fertility. If possible, cast the spell on Beltane (May 1) for extra energy. First, poke a pencil-sized hole in the side of the egg so you can drain its contents completely. Next, gently break away a little more (so there's an opening large enough for the seeds to easily pass through). Rinse with cool water and let the egg dry inside before enacting the spell.

Light your candle and take a deep cleansing breath, in through your nose and out through your mouth. Imagine the area of your life in question being as fertile as you need (need drives magick—desire is good, but need is less greedy). Take your time here. Let the imagery play itself out completely. The more complete the image, the better chances of specific manifestation. Finally, take the seeds and slowly begin filling the eggshell saying:

"The light of hope shines.
What I wish for can be mine.
This seed I plant shall root and grow.
As within so without; as above, so below!"

Finally, take the seeded shell and put it in rich soil and tend it regularly. Let the candle burn out naturally or, if possible, put it in the soil above the egg. By the time the seeds sprout, you should notice similar changes in your reality.

This spell is specifically for a couple wishing to conceive a child. If possible, wait until the moon is full (but if that's not when your cycle is fertile, obviously adjust accordingly). Begin by decorating the sleeping chamber with romantic candles including one white one to represent the spirit of the unborn child. Dress in something pleasing to your partner and wear a musky aromatic.

Leave the child's candle unlit on a table near the bed. Adjacent to that candle, lay a piece of yellow (creation's color) string or yarn. Sit down and join hands with your partner. Light the candle and speak into the flame all the hopes and wishes you have for the future (specifically why you want to be parents). If it is possible to leave this candle lit safely throughout the love-making process, I strongly recommend it—the light represents life! Keep the string near your heart. Remember to follow up with your physician in about a month.

Finding (Discovery)

These spells are rather like the Sherlock Holmes of the spiritual world. When you've misplaced your car keys, lost a special piece of jewelry, can't remember who borrowed your favorite CD, or need to discover some other elusive bits of information, this is a great place to start.

* Time your spells for when the first signs of a new moon begin to evidence in the sky. Alternatively, wait until the moon is in Libra to restore the balance.

* Add aromatics such as apple, allspice, lilac, and sandalwood, which improve both conscious and subconscious awareness and insights.

* Use a candle whose color represents the item lost somehow. For example, if you lost your wallet and it was brown, use a brown candle (or a green one to symbolize the money within).

⁂ Include other potential components and symbols such as knots (to hold on to things that might be lost), the letter X (X marks the spot), the number four (Earth-oriented), a dousing rod, pendulum, magnets (to attract), and a boomerang shaped item.

This first spell helps when you've dropped an item and have a vague idea of the area in which it may have gotten away from you (like between two houses, in a park, etc.). It requires a candle (any color but white for clarity might be a good choice) and a pendulum. Also, if you can gather some dirt from the area in which you lost the item, even better.

Light the candle saying:

"Light my way. Guide my steps.
"Let what was lost be found,
above, below, or on the ground."

Carefully pick up the candle and allow a little of the wax to drip into the dirt, and then put another small dab on the chain or point of the pendulum. Caution: Use only a very small amount. Any more can skew the pendulum by its weight alone.

Next, go to the area in which you lost the item. Start in the middle and work outward in clockwise circles and stop at every "hour" point. Each time you stop, steady the pendulum and mentally or orally repeat the original incantation. Watch for the pendulum to move. If it seems to move up and down, keep moving forward on the line you're on rather than the circles. If it moves in a circle, check the ground where you stand. If that yields no results, then continue in the circular path. Sometimes the pendulum will seem to have a stronger motion to one direction (the upswing or downswing). If this happens likewise follow in that direction. Remember to keep an image of the lost item in your mind's eye the whole time you work.

This next spell is a simple revision of an old folk spell. For it, you'll need three pieces of yarn (one white, one yellow, and one that represents the lost item) each about four inches long, a picture of the lost item, and a candle. Light the candle, and begin to braid these strands together focusing all your attention on the lost item. Say:

"Three by three, return to me!"

Continue to whisper this incantation throughout the braiding process.

Next, take the image of the item and wrap the string around it so that it's securely tied within. Put this on the table just beyond the candle holding the other end of the braided string in your hand. Slowly pull the image closer to you, continuing to repeat the same incantation all the while. When the picture reaches your hands, wrap all the braided yarn around it, and secure it with a bit of melted wax. Keep this in a safe place until the item manifests or a replacement comes your way.

Focus

The ability to maintain your attention for extended periods of time is not simply a skill for metaphysicians. It's also a skill that helps students, teachers, professionals, and athletes alike (just to name a few). Magickally speaking, however, without the ability to focus, all the energy built by a spell, charm, or ritual can simply dissipate or go awry. No one wants that! So, when you feel like your ability to stay on track is getting derailed, try these candlelight spells (then work the more intense magicks afterward!)

* Time your spells according to the area of your life in which you need more focus. For example,

a full moon supports efforts for improved religious or spiritual attention.

❄ Add aromatics such as coffee (known for its ability to "wake" us up).

❄ Use any candle, but white might be best for all-purpose attentiveness. Alternatively, yellow is the color of the conscious mind.

❄ Include other potential components and symbols such as a magnifying glass, a cross hairs (which draws our attention to a specific point), a bell (the sound has strong centering qualities) and a ring (to border the item toward which you're focusing like a frame).

This spell requires a symbol of the area of your life where you need focus drawn on a small piece of paper, an inexpensive 3 x 5 frame, and a candle of your choice. If you wish, dab the candle with some perked coffee before you begin. Light the candle and put your hands palm down over the piece of paper. Remember that in magick a symbol is just as potent as what it represents. Next, add an incantation like:

"Hocus-Pocus, I need FOCUS."

While this sounds amusing, it's very easy to remember (and that's important—you'll see why in a minute).

Next, dab all four corners of the frame with some wax drippings from the candle. Start with the upper right corner saying:

"Air, Fire, Water, Earth—combine.
Let my focus be refined!"

Put the paper into the frame then pick out a location in your house where you can see it several times a day. Each time you see the frame, repeat the first (or second) invocation to support the magick.

This next spell should be enacted when you get up in the morning over your cup of coffee (or tea, or whatever your "wake me up" beverage is). Dab a little rosemary oil on your candle to improve your conscious mind for the day. Light it. Then with a spoon, stir your beverage clockwise saying:

> *"Within this beverage I bind,*
> *focus for my conscious mind.*
> *When taken to my lips,*
> *the magick's released in every sip!"*

Enjoy the beverage at a leisurely pace, letting the focus settle in like a warm, centered feeling near your navel. Go out and greet your day!

Forgiveness

As the saying goes, to forgive is divine. Nonetheless, humans have not fully realized their divine nature yet— it's sometimes hard for us to forgive. We cling to our memories and pains like badges of honor, even when there's no real purpose any longer for such a display. Forgiveness heals and opens the door for many other positive things. That's where Candle Magick comes in handy.

* Time your spells for when the moon is in Libra (for fairness), a new moon, dawn, or spring (for a fresh start), or Friday (the traditional day for "relationship" work).

* Add aromatics such as lavender for peace, mint to clear the air, lemon to encourage friendly feelings, and violet to heal the damage done.

❄ Use blue candles for peace, or white to symbolize the truce.

❄ Include other potential components and symbols such as amethyst, which regulates your personal temperament, white clothing (again to imply truce), blue tourmaline or sodalite (peace), ice (for cooling off), or salve (for healing and recovery).

This mini ritual requires that everyone involved be present (or minimally contribute something personal to the ritual to show their good intention). Each person should bring a candle that represents himself or herself to the sacred space. There should be one large white candle on the altar.

As each person enters the Circle, they put their candle (in a holder) around the white candle, and light it, saying:

"I bring the light of truth, and a heart of peace."

After lighting the personal candle, put your hands up (as if surrendering), saying:

"I bring no ill will,
Nor will my words be used as weapons.
I join this Circle of healing freely."

Take your place in the Circle.

Once each person has done this, you should pass a talking stick around the circle counter clockwise (for banishing) to give each person to say their peace and provide perspectives. If it needs to go around several times to clear things up, do so. Note that while one person is speaking, no one else may interrupt until they have the talking stick. This avoids confusion.

Once everything is settled, everyone should approach the altar and pick up their individual candles. These are lit to the main white candle chanting together:

"Hostility and misunderstandings have ceased;
We promise ourselves to peace!"

This chant should be repeated one time for each person present (but said in unison). Blow out the individual candles. Take some of the wax from the central white one and drip it on to each person's candle so they can take home group unity and keep that candle on their altar.

This second forgiveness spell requires that each participant bring one black and one white candle into the sacred space. Each person in turn should light their black candle and speak honestly about the issues on their hearts and minds. This is the time to pour the sadness, remaining anger, and any other negativity into that candle's flame. All other participants should remain silent—this is a purging period for the individual, but also a good time to hone your listening skills so that similar situations don't occur in the future.

Continue until each person has had a turn, then all in unison should blow out and break their black candles into thirds (for forgiveness on all levels of Being). These shards get dumped into a garbage receptacle. Finally, as before, each person lights their personal white candle and talks of their hopes for the future. This part of the spell/ritual is limited to only positive insights and goal. Let the candles burn for a while so everyone can sit and talk in the light of peace. Take these home and light them any time you start getting angry about those things which have already been set aside.

Freedom

Freedom is a small word with huge significance. As people who practice a "alternative ideology/religion," freedom is very important to the broad-based Neo-Pagan community. On a personal level, our ability to choose freely for ourselves is so essential to a healthy human outlook and approach to life. When you feel that someone or something is limiting those freedoms that we hold dear, work with these spells.

※ Time your spells for when the sun is clearly shining (truth and freedom do not hide in shadows).

※ Add aromatics that are very light (nothing overpowering).

※ Use a candle whose color represents the area of your life in which you need freedom. Alternatively use black to banish constraint.

※ Include other potential components and symbols that represent liberation such as broken knots or a butterfly.

I have a great fondness for Knot Magick. For this spell, you'll need a 5-6' length of sturdy rope (something weather resistant) and a candle. You'll also need 12 small items that you can bind into the rope that represent the area of your life where restrictions exist. Light your candle, saying:

"Let the light of freedom shine in my heart and my life. Today I claim liberation from_____. I will it, I deserve it, it is mine—so mote it be!"

Next, take the 12 items and bind each one into *one* knot with some of the wax drippings, saying:

"As you have held me, now I hold you. As each knot is untied, _____'s influence over me wanes."

Next, take this rope and hang it up outside. Once a day, starting on the third day of the full moon to the dark moon, untie *one* knot. Typically this will leave one knot in the rope (which should remain there to keep the restrictive energy bound). Keep the rope someplace safe until complete liberation is achieved. Then burn or bury both the rope and the token with the candle.

⸙

This next meditation requires only a candle and a good imagination. Take your candle to a quiet, comfortable place where you can sit in front of it. Carve the image of a butterfly close to the top of the candle before you light it. Sit and watch the candle's flame liberate the butterfly's image from the wax. Breathe deeply, then close your eyes and see that butterfly in your mind's eye. Its image grows larger and larger until it superimposes itself on your aura. If you move your arms, its wings move with you.

Let yourself become that butterfly. Lift yourself above where you're sitting now, above your circumstances. Feel the release…see with a larger perspective. Let the transformational energy of Butterfly Spirit give you the hope and help you need to break free from whatever holds you back. Fly with the butterfly as long as you wish, then open your eyes and focus on the candle once more. Breathe normally and ground yourself, then blow out the candle. Keep it for similar meditations in the future.

Friendship

"Acquaintance without patience
is like a candle with no light."

—Iranian Proverb

The value of good friends should never be underestimated. Our friends stay true even when the world itself seems to be going completely crazy. Thus, these spells are designed to strengthen the friendships you have, heal those where there might be misunderstandings, or bring the right people into your life who have the potential of taking on that very special role.

❄ Time your spells for Spring (the season of growth), when the moon is in Aquarius, waxing or full moons, or on a special date that commemorates a friendship's beginning.

❄ Add aromatics such as sweet pea or lemon, both of which nurture gentle love.

❄ Use candles that are your friend's favorite color. Alternatively, to attract a friend, pink is a good choice.

❄ Include other potential components and symbols such as pale-colored jade, for comradery, and friendship rings.

This mini ritual inspired ongoing ties, warm feelings, communication, and rapport between two or more people. For it, each person needs a pink candle, pictures of your friend(s) or a personal item from them, and a toothpick. Use the toothpick to carve the name(s) of the individual(s) involved in the ritual. Dab the carving with a bit of lemon juice and perhaps some rose oil (another good love aroma).

Come the next waxing moon, each of you puts the pink candle and the picture(s) together in a special spot. I like to use a window to symbolize sending light out into the world to touch my friends. At the same time of day (one where you know all of you can be home), each person involved lights his or her candle. Make sure to focus on the picture(s) of your friend(s) as it helps guide the energy. When the match ignites the wick, add an incantation such as:

"Far or near, away or here,
I hold_____in my heart as dear."

Fill in the blank with the name(s) of your friend(s). Repeat this ritual until the moon is full. Then, if possible, get together that night (before the moon begins to wane) so the magick takes stronger root.

This is a fun divination to try with any number of your friends. Gather together whenever you can and have each person bring a spare candle from other divinatory work (it doesn't matter what color, so long as the focus was divination). You'll also need a 10 x 12 piece of sturdy art paper. (If you have a lot of people coming, increase the size of the paper accordingly. The 10 x 12 works for three people, four if you scrunch.)

Put the paper on a flat surface and your candles around it (each lit by it's owner). Everyone join hands and think about your friendship—all your hopes and dreams for each other. Wait until you feel the tingle of energy in the air or the temperature rise a bit and release hands. Each participant then picks up his or her candle, and tips it over the white paper from where they stand. Carefully walk clockwise around the table keeping the candle over the paper. When you've gone around three times, stop, and let the wax cool.

Afterward, scry the results looking for patterns or even an entire picture. Each person should share what they see in the imagery. Then cut the whole thing up into equal segments so everyone can take a piece home and keep it as a symbol of the ongoing friendship and ties between all those gathered.

Gossip (halting)

Tired of people who have no lives of their own and therefore talk about everyone else's? Me too! I suspect nearly everyone reading this book has been the victim of gossip at least once and knows how harmful it can be. The purpose behind gossip spells is to encourage the mill to stop. While we can't directly influence free will, we can encourage honesty and an improved awareness of the potential outcomes from such dialogues. That's where these spells begin.

- ❋ Time your spells for dark moons (the time of least activity to really weed out the whole issue). Or for when the moon is in Libra to restore balance.
- ❋ Add aromatics such as pine for cleansing, fennel to purify and heal, or rosemary and lilac for clarity.
- ❋ Use a white candle for honesty, or a black one for banishing. Alternatively, use a yellow candle to represent communication.
- ❋ Include other potential components and symbols for truth, some of which are bluebells, eyebright, sunflower, and carnelian.

Gather together the following components for this spell: a piece of paper (large enough to write a brief description of the problem), a pen (green ink for healing is one idea), a candle of your choosing, and a clothespin. Put your candle on a tabletop where you can also write. Light it, saying:

"I claim the light of truth. I claim the fires of cleansing.
I claim the warmth of honest friends.
I claim liberty from lies."

Now write down the area of your life that's been affected by gossip. Think of all the details you know as you write, but you need not include them all—just something simple and symbolic. Drip some of the wax on the four corners of the papers saying (starting in the upper right):

"By the Power of Air,
the winds of rumors shall die down and cease.
By the Power of Fire,

people's minds will see the light of truth.
By the Power of Water,
I shall know healing.
By the Power of Earth, there will be renewal."

Finally, take the paper, the clip, and the candle outside. Put the clip on a clothesline (or something similar) with the paper inside. Ignite the paper and let it burn to ashes (released to the four winds). Let the candle likewise burn itself out so that all the energy dissipates.

This combination divination helps you uncover the source of a rumor. You'll need a large diameter candle (the color is your choice but I suggest a blue one for truth), a large piece of paper (16 x 22 is good), a plastic garbage bag, and a marker or pen. All over the paper, in no particular placement, write down all the potential sources of the rumor based on the information you've gathered thus far. Cut open the plastic bag so it covers the surface where you're putting the paper, and lay the paper on top (this protects your countertops or tables from hot wax).

Next, light the candle saying:

"Secrets in the fire reveal, while the liquid wax congeals.
Lies are like an open book,
show me...show me where to look."

Continue to repeat this incantation until there is a good puddle of wax on the surface of the candle (1/8"—1/4" deep). Hold this slightly above the paper while standing or sitting so you can see the whole sheet from a central location. Blow *gently* on the wax so it spatters on the surface of the paper (this gives life to your magick).

Finally, look to see where the wax landed. You'll often find lines (implying a direction in which to look), blobs right on top of one or two people, and so forth. If there are no specific indicators, look at the pattern as a whole for more insights.

Grounding (Foundations)

There's a lot about magick and spirituality that is based in faith. Thus, keeping one foot firmly planted in reality is a pretty wise idea. Additionally, by doing so you give your-self strong foundations in which energy can root and grow. These candlelit efforts are geared toward that purpose:

❋ Time your spells for the dark moon (tradi-tionally when one weeds the garden or lets the soil rest). Spring is also a good time (plant-ing season), as are times when the moon is in Capricorn, or Thursdays.

❋ Add aromatics with a strong Earthy overtone such as patchouli and vetiver, the latter of which inspires transformation and manifestation.

❋ Use brown or black candles (the colors of rich soil).

❋ Include other potential components and sym-bols such as seeds, dirt, in-ground vegetables (carrots, potatoes), and other symbols of strong foundations with roots. Additionally, stones like obsidian, concrete, and onyx are known for their good grounding qualities.

Spells

When you feel that you just can't seem to keep one foot on the ground or regain your mundane sense of center after a difficult ritual try this activity. You'll need a brown or black candle and some anointing oil that reminds you of the Earth (I use a woodland blend). Sit as close to the ground as possible with the candle in front of you and both hands on the floor or ground. Light it and focus all your excessive, "flighty" energy into the flame. Let that energy flow. You may find that you actually start to feel heavier. This is a good sign.

Take a drop of the anointing oil you've chosen and carefully dab it near to the top of the candle. Then take a little more on your pointer finger and apply it to the bottoms of your feet saying:

> *"Down, down, onto the ground.*
> *Stay firmly footed, safe and sound!"*

If possible, keep some of this oil with you and use it as aromatherapy anytime you feel yourself starting to loose that sense of center. To activate the aromatic aspect, just dab it on pulse points and your shoes, and repeat the incantation.

For this spell you'll need a crystal of your choice, a place to work outside undisturbed on the last night of the dark moon, and a candle. Put the candle into a sturdy holder on the ground. Stand in front of it holding the crystal you've brought with you in your strong hand. Direct your eyes to the candle's flame. Think about the area of your life that needs more foundational energy in as much detail as possible. Feel how connected your feet are to the ground at this moment—how steady the candle is on the ground. The Earth has always been here. It's not going anywhere, and it's the perfect place to give anything roots.

Take your time meditating in this manner until you feel the crystal in your hand growing warm. Put it up to your heart chakra and say:

> *"The needs, hopes, and dreams of my heart are grounded*
> *in the Earth,*
> *where they will root and grow."*

Bend down and put the crystal in the soil right near the candle. Let the candle burn out of its own accord. Leave the crystal in the dirt. As long as it's there that part of your life will hold firm. Warning: Do not leave this where animals are likely to dig, thereby uprooting the energy.

Happiness

"She would rather light a candle than curse the darkness, and her glow has warmed the world."

—Adlai Stevenson

Health and happiness are two of the key things that all mothers wish for their children and extended family. When you have joy as a companion, it's much easier to cope with life's chaos and periodic troubles. Nonetheless, there are times when we feel sad or down in the dumps. The causes vary, but these spells will help affect a cure!

* Time your spells for any day when the sun is shining (a symbol of joy and blessings). Additionally the season of Spring provides hopeful, upbeat energy toward this goal.
* Add aromatics such as catnip, chrysanthemum, lotus, orange, mint, or thyme all of which can improve our mood. Alternatively, think of the scents that bring back happy memories.
* Use light blue candles.
* Include other potential components and symbols such as a feather (tickle your fancy), anything with bubbles, berries (an abundant joy), and cat's eye, which is said to bring happiness to the bearer.

The next time you're feeling sad, gather together a bottle of sparkling apple cider, some raspberries, and a bright blue candle. Work near a sunny window where there's a surface that you can use for food preparation. Set a bowl of the berries in the sunlight right next to the unlit blue candle saying:

"The light of the sun is that of thousands of candles.
Let it shine in my heart and chase all shadows."

Open the bottle of sparkling cider, pour a little over the berries, and stir them clockwise with your finger, saying:

"To me, in me, happiness to me!"

Consume with a hopeful heart. By the way, the candle was not lit in this spell because an old country custom dictates that you should not light a hearth when the sun shines on it. The Fire spirits are sometimes jealous of each other.

This mini-ritual takes one week to enact, starting on the waxing moon and going thru to the full moon. For it, I'd like to suggest a spectrum of candles going from red to violet, in the order of the rainbow. Having the blue and purple at the end of the line encourages both joy and wisdom. Carve images of the things that will make you the most happy, one each, into the candles. Try and match these goals with the candle's color (such as a heart on the red one, a dollar sign on the green one, and so forth).

On the first day, you'll light the red candle and say the first verse of the following incantation once. On the second day, you'll light the red and orange candle and repeat the first and second verse *twice*. On the third day, you light the red, orange, and yellow candle and repeat the first through *third* verses three times. This continues throughout the seven days:

"Red brings me energy to weather the storms.
Orange is the harvest, of good karma and just rewards.

Yellow is the winds of change, stirring about.
Green is the first sign of Spring and hope—
without a doubt!
Blue is for what I wish most, unbridled happiness.
Indigo is for the wisdom to cherish those things with which
I'm blessed.
Violet, is for the spirit within, and without to ignite.
With magick, with joy, beginning tonight!"

The last two lines are a couplet added the seventh night. Let the candles burn each night for a few minutes while you visualize the goal etched into that candle being manifested. On the last night, make sure the candles all burn down to the point where they release your mark. You can then blow them out and reuse the rest.

Hauntings (Ghosts)

Things that go bump in the night can keep life interesting or cause disruption. When you think you may have an unruly ghost, here are some magickal ideas for finding out (a) if it's really present, (b) why, and (c) how to get rid of that energy if you so choose:

※ Time your spells for the full moon or midnight, or other times when the spirit world is thought to be active akin to Beltane, Lammas, and Samhain.

※ Add aromatics such as sweet grass, chrysanthemum, heather, and violet (all associated with spirits of the dead).

※ Use a white candle or a candle whose color somehow represents the ghost's personality and demeanor.

※ Include other potential components and symbols trusted for their ability to call spirits such

as dandelion, thistle, salt and iron (protective), and azurite or lapis to improve your
psychic sensitivity.

This activity uses a candle to determine if the presence of a ghost exists and if so, in what main area of a
house or room. I suggest a plain candle without any carvings
or aromatics. Wait for a suitable time to work (preferably at
night). Begin in the area where you feel you typically sense the
spirit. Make sure there are no open windows, drafts, or other
interruptions.

Put the candle on a flat surface and light it. Watch for the
following signs that traditionally indicate the presence of a spirit:

* The wax melts down one side and curves
  around (this is called a winding sheet).
* The flame of the candle seems brighter on
  one side than the other (this means the
  ghost is closer to that spot).
* The flame gets blown out by a cold breeze
  (note the direction for more insights to
  narrow down the general region).

These beliefs are very old and have a long tradition on
which to base your observations. Make notes of what you
experience, where, and when. Keep this log until a pattern
arises, then use that pattern to gather more information.

This spell is designed to protect you from ghosts if you
feel you need it (to be honest, living with them can be far
more interesting!). You'll need several votive candles (one
for every window in the room where you feel the ghost's
presence. Additionally, bring a white taper candle and a red
ribbon or piece of yarn. Begin in a northward window, placing one votive there and lighting it saying:

"Home is my sacred space;
Malicious spirit be gone from this place."

Repeat this process with all the other windows.

Next, stand in the middle of the room holding the remaining white taper. Tie the red ribbon or yarn near the middle of the taper, repeating this incantation three times:

"Around this candle red ribbon wind, by my will this
spirit—BIND!"

Keep the candle carefully stored away and only light it during times when you feel the negativity returning. The votives should be allowed to burn out (they do not drip so wax won't be an issue. Just make sure there aren't any nearby curtains).

Finally, what if you wish to make contact with spirits? There are times when we want to welcome them among us (such as commemorating a deceased loved one's birthday). There are other times we'd like their insights. In this case, light a candle to represent the spirit you're welcoming (perhaps dab it with some of the person's favorite cologne or perfume). Place this across from that person's picture on a table.

You'll also need the name of the person written on parchment. This is put midway between the candle and the picture. Now, focus on your desire to spend time with that spirit. Take the pointer finger of your strong hand and trace a path from the picture to the parchment saying:

"I open the door to you and only you.
_____be welcome in my home and sacred space."

Fill in the blank with the name of the person, then pick up the scroll in your hand. Use this to finish tracing the path to the candle and ignite the parchment. Note: Be sure to have a fire-safe container (for example, a stoneware bowl filled with sand or dirt and placed on a trivet) into which you can put the parchment while it burns. Visualize the face of the person in the flame of the candle, saying:

"As this parchment burns away, so do the barriers between my world and thine.
I open the door to you and only you. Be welcome."

From here, what happens usually varies. You may sense a presence, smell a unique aroma, hear something, or even have no experience whatsoever until you go to sleep that night and dream! Keep your eyes open and remain aware of subtle clues that your guest has arrived.

Healing/Health

Typically, I suggest that you have someone else perform healing spells or rituals when you're ailing. No matter how adept one may be, some of the negative energy from sickness can taint our magick. Also, if you do choose to enact a healing spell for someone, make sure you have permission. All the magick in the world won't help someone recover if they don't want to get better! Should it be impossible to get permission, then work the spell in such a way that you leave the energy open for acceptance or rejection by the intended recipient.

As a side note, Babylonians considered candlelight Divine medicine!

 ❊ Time your spells for a waning moon to banish sickness or a waxing moon to encourage recovery. Also working in sunlight improves well-being.

❋ Add aromatics such as fennel, mint, apple, or orange, all of which are associated with a sound body, mind, and spirit.

❋ Use pale (shoot) green candles (the color of new growth), or white (for purification).

❋ Include other potential components and symbols that represent health or healing to you. For example, I enjoy making a chicken soup potion in combination with my healing spells. Other options include: salves, bandages, a first aid kit, and so forth.

For this spell, I recommend you choose the candle's color to represent the disorder. Anoint this with lavender and rose oil, which encourages peace and self-love (or love toward the person for whom the spell has been designed). If possible, also have a token to represent the ill person so you can better direct the energy (a photograph is one idea, or something they've given you over the years).

Put the candle on a small table around which you can walk easily. Light the candle and hold the item that represents the ill person. Walk counterclockwise around the table eight times, repeating this incantation once on every complete circuit:

"To the Earth, to the Earth, all negativity to Earth.
To earth to Earth, all sickness to Earth.
_____Accept this spell, become well!"

Fill in the blank with the name of the person toward whom the energy is intended. Note: There is a clause here that allows the individual to *accept* or *reject* the energy, thereby not stepping over free will guidelines.

Upon completion, either let the candle burn itself out and bury the remains (in the earth as you have commanded the sickness) or, wrap the candle in a soft cloth and keep it in a safe place to protect the person until they recover.

For this spell you'll require a candle (in the color of your choice), a small piece of paper, a pen, a fireproof container, and some cleansing oil like cedar. On the piece of paper, write the name of the malady near the top. Now, underneath that word, write it again but leave off the last letter. Continue to rewrite (subtracting another letter each time) in this way until there is only one letter in the malady left (it looks like an inverted triangle).

Next, light the candle and dab the final point of the triangle with the oil. Focus on cleansing away every last vestige of the malady from whomever is ailing. Light the paper on fire and transfer it to the fireproof container, continuing to focus on your goal until the paper is completely consumed. Take the ashes outside and release them to the winds to complete the process.

Holidays

Throughout the year, there are celebrations and festivals to which candles bring their lovely glow and ambiance. While it would be impossible to cover every holiday in a book like this, I would like to share with you some ways in which candles have traditionally been utilized at holiday settings. Because this theme is unique, I can't provide broad-based timing, aromatics, and colors (each holiday is different). Rather, I'm going to give you a list of dates, description of the celebration, how candles were and are used, and what they symbolize, so that you can consider doing similar things on those dates (or using that timing to accent other magickal efforts).

- ❆ January—Carnival: A pre-lent, European festival that includes large candles as a form of celebration and merrymaking before the more serious season begins.
- ❆ February 2—Candlemas: This is a celebration of light triumphing over darkness, and is

intended to give the sun strength to return to full power after Winter.

✻ March 31—Feast of the Moon Goddess: A festival that comes from Rome. The tradition is to light 13 candles today to honor the moons of the year.

✻ April (early)—Boat Festival in France: On this day, people place small candles in boats along with their wishes!

✻ April 8—Buddha's birthday: Light eight candles on this day to encourage enlightenment and serenity in your own life.

✻ May 3—Bon Dea: Roman celebration of abundance. If you jump a candle on this day, it brings good fortune.

✻ June 21—Summer Solstice: Light any candle on this day to honor the sun in all its glory.

✻ August 15—Birthday of Isis: Lighting a candle on this day encourages blessings for those who travel frequently.

✻ September 25—Festival of Durga Puja: This Indian goddess safeguards our home and those we love, and can be invoked on this day using a yellow candle.

✻ October 31—Halloween: What would any Hallows celebration be without a candle in a pumpkin to protect us from evil spirits?

✻ November 16—Diwali: Indian festival honoring the goddess of wealth. You can encourage her favor by lighting yellow or gold colored candles on this day.

✻ December 21—Yule: A festival of lights (similar to Candlemas) with a stronger focus on the hearth and home. Candles are lit to

honor Nature spirits who keep trees like
evergreens alive through the harsh months.

Humor

Laughter is good soul food and humor a great coping mechanism for life's bumps and bruises. The problem is that our daily routines can quickly rob us of this very important attribute just from wear and tear alone. When you feel your sense of humor waning, keep these things in mind for candlelit activities.

❊   Time your spells for whenever you're feeling
unamused. I wouldn't wait for things to get worse.

❊   Add light aromatics (humor shouldn't have
heavy energy) that you personally enjoy (it's
hard to be upbeat when you hate what you're
smelling).

❊   Use a multi-colored candle if you can find
one. I personally see humor as a rainbow-like
glitter that sprinkles into one's aura. The
multi-colored candle reflects that idea.

❊   Include other potential components and symbols such as a feather to tickle your fancy and
good jokes and puns in the ritual. Also
bubbles, balloons, and anything else that
wakes up the inner child's sense of whimsy.

Choose a candle that's to your liking and find a feather. If you find the feather outside, however, please put it in a plastic bag in the freezer for one week to kill off any insect hitchhikers. Place the candle on a surface where you can see it easily when standing. Light the candle and breathe deeply. Really try to relax and loosen up—it's nearly impossible to be humorous when your over-wound.

Next, brush the feather through all of your aura (your head, arms, torso, legs, and even below your feet). As you do chant this little ditty:

"Negativity take flight; tickled by light
Negativity flee; good humor restore in me!"

Afterward, let the candle continue to burn (if its safe to do so) and go do something fun that will really inspire your funny bone (maybe go to a comedy club or rent your favorite humorous movie).

Inspiration

"We owe a lot to Thomas Edison—if it wasn't for him, we'd be watching television by candlelight."

—Milton Berle

What is a world without the muse—without that wonderful bit of starlight and moonbeam that touches our pen, paints, carvings, or random moments with inspiration? Nonetheless, Many days I wouldn't know inspiration if it walked up and tapped me on one shoulder! When you feel similarly, and want to refill the well of creativity, begin here.

❄ Time your spells for when the moon is in Cancer, the waxing moon, the month of April (and all of Spring), or days when the wind is blowing gently (so that ideas can take flight).

❄ Add aromatics such as allspice and lotus, both known to manifest the muse.

❄ Use yellow or silver candles (or another color you associate with creativity).

❄ Include other potential components and symbols such as a lamp (ideas), mad (for inventive words), stars (wishes), and quartz for productivity.

To encourage inspiration into a project or art form, bring the main tools of that project or art to your altar or another special spot where they can remain undisturbed. Do this on the first night of the full moon, placing the items in the light of three candles (one for each night of the full moon). On the first night, light the first candle, saying:

"Tonight the moon is full,
So too fill my mind and spirit with ideas.
As this candle burns bright,
Ignite the spark of inspiration within."

Blow out the candle and sit, meditating in the moonlight for a while undisturbed.

On the second night, light the first candle repeating the first incantation. Then light the second candle from the first, saying:

"As one flame to the other,
So too does the light of inspiration spread to my soul."

Blow out that candle and spend more time in quiet meditation.

On the last night, light the first and second candle repeating their invocations as before. Then light the third from the second saying:

"As I will it, so mote it be.
The flame of inspiration I claim—it burns within me!"

By the way, you may wish to take a notebook with you into the first two night's meditation. A lot of people say they get ideas during that time.

Tonight, leave the candles burning and do some work with the items you've left on the surface, absorbing your magick.

This spell is for general inspiration. To begin, it you'll need a candle and a feather. You will also need to enact it in a place where that you can release the feather to a live water source ("live" meaning moving). Sit down near the water and light your candle. Hold the feather, cupping it in both hands. Bring the feather to your heart chakra and visualize the area of your life in which you desire greater inspiration. Put that desire in the form of a wish that you state out loud. For example, if I wanted more inspiration in my writing I would say:

"This feather is as the quill of my pen.
As it's touched by the Fire, so too touch my heart.
As it's released to living waters,
Let the waves of inspiration flow to me and through me."

For inspiration in a business plan, I might say:

"This feather is the lifting wing of my work.
As it's touched by the Fire, so too give light to my plans.
As it's released to the vibrant waves,
So too let the Waters of creativity fill my work."

Continue holding the feather close until you feel it completely saturated with your will. Put the tip into the fire so that it sparks, then release it immediately to the water so the flow can take your wishes to the world. Blow out the candle and keep it for other creativity-oriented spells.

꙳ ꙰ ꙳

When you need to overcome some type of blockage (typically discouragement or self-doubt) in order to feel more inspired again, this is a good spell to enact. For it, you will need one candle to represent you, one black candle (to represent the blockage), and one candle to represent the area of your life in which you're feeling halted. Carve each candle with symbols suited to its function. For example, if the blockage is in matters of love, carve a heart on the third candle (perhaps a red one). Carve your initials into your candle.

Set up the candles on the table in a line with the black candle in the middle of the three (it represents the blockage—now you have a visual image of that). This candle will not be lit (you don't want to give more power to the problems). Rather light *your* candle first, saying:

> *"Even as dawn breaks the night and becomes day,*
> *no more does this problem stand in my way!"*

Keep repeating this incantation until you feel your confidence growing naturally. Reach out with your strong hand and remove the black candle from between the other two and break it. Put it aside.

Finally, light the last candle, saying:

> *"My will and my resolve are sure.*
> *From the flame of my heart,*
> *I light a new fire under_____*
> *and reclaim inspiration."*

Fill in the blank with the area of your life where inspiration has been lacking. If possible, let these candles burn out of their own accord.

Jealousy

Jealousy is among the most destructive and unproductive emotions in humankind. It can completely tear apart long-term relationships, cause dissention among friends or families, and eat away at a person's spirit like a cancer. There is a large difference between caring about someone and thinking of him or her as a personal possession. Similarly, even when there may be a good reason for feeling a little envious or mistrustful, it is always good to take a few steps back to try to gain more perspective. These candle activities give you a few ways to readjust your outlooks and bring positive energy to bear:

* Time your spells for the waning or dark moon, dusk, or when the moon is in Aries (cleaning out old habits) or Libra (restoring balance).

* Add aromatics such as mint and violet that both clear the air and restore peace.

* Use green candles to represent the jealousy, or white for purifying intention.

* Include other potential components and symbols that represent the individual from whom the jealousy originates, or carnelian, which improves communication skills and stills jealousy.

This first spell is designed to halt unwarranted jealousy aimed at you. To enact it, you must be certain of the source of the problem. Gather together a white candle, a piece of paper, a pen, an ice cube tray, and water. If possible, wait until the waning moon (to shrink the negative energy). Write the source of jealousy on the paper (perhaps in green ink). Light the candle, saying:

"No need for possessiveness; no need for ill will
By this spell, your jealousy CHILL!"

Fold the paper in half, then in half again, and in half again (three times all told) and then seal it with candle wax. Put it in the ice cube tray with water and freeze. Leave this in the back of the freezer for as long as necessary to cool down the problem.

By the way, you can enact this spell for yourself if you're the one having overly possessive tendencies (and harboring ill will because of them).

This spell requires a greenish-yellow candle, a cup of water, and a carnelian stone. Put the stone in the cup of water and set it aside. Light the candle and focus all your jealousy into it. Think of all the situations that make you feel jealous. Consider exactly how you feel in those moments. Let all that energy pour into the candle's flame. Now, carefully pick up the candle in your strong hand and look at it saying:

> *"Jealousy has no power over me.*
> *It's control I quell*
> *By my will and this spell!"*

Turn the candle upside down and douse it in the water. Throw away the candle to disengage yourself from the jealousy. Keep the water-bathed stone as a talisman. Any time you feel the green-eyed monster creeping back, hold the stone in your hand and repeat the incantation to yourself.

Justice (legal matters)

Are you facing a problem with lawyers? Do you have to sign a complex contract? Do you feel as if people or circumstances have trampled any sense of equity, truth, and fairness? I know I've faced each one of these situations and have felt as if I had no voice or power. There are times when red tape binds you mundanely, but, magickally, it holds no strength. These spells can serve as scissors cutting through the issues you may be facing in this arena:

❋ Time your spells for when the Moon is in Libra, Tuesdays, or when the sun is shining brightly.

❋ Add aromatics such as ash wood (as an incense base) and vanilla.

❋ Use a white or gold candle.

❈   Include other potential components and
    symbols such as carnelian, the Justice card
    of the tarot, hematite, a gavel, scales, and
    amethyst (for tempering energies).

Gather together a gold candle, some finely-ground
wood, and a vanilla bean finely shaved. Put the candle in
the center of a bowl filled with dirt or sand, then sprinkle
the wood and vanilla around it. Each day, rub a little of
the wood and bean into the candle and light it. Take a
moment and think about the problem that requires justice. Visualize it resolved in the best, most positive way.
Leave the candle to burn while you prepare for your day,
then blow it out before leaving. Continue this mini-ritual
every day until the problem ceases. Note: If you have to
replace the candle during this time, light the new candle
from the flame of the first, then put the bottom of the new
one into some of the melted wax from the previous. This
"builds" the energy by making an unbroken line of wax.

　　　　　　　　　⚬ ⟨⟨❧ ❦⟩⟩ ⚬

This bit of magick requires a tiny candle (like those
for a birthday cake), a pouch, and a carnelian. During the
noon hour, go outside with the candle and the carnelian
and bless them, saying:

"Spirit, shine the light of truth and fairness upon me.
When I ignite this candle,
Let all around see clearly through the darkness.
When I touch this stone,
let my words be clear and understood
so that there will be a fair resolution."

Put the candle and stone into the pouch and keep it with
you for a suitable moment. Excuse yourself and go to the lava-
tory to light the candle briefly. Repeat your prayer mentally,

directing your energy toward this specific situation (add more information if you feel it prudent). Then take out the stone and put it in your pocket. Blow out the candle (put a little water on the tip before replacing it in the pouch so it won't burn the fabric). Finally, return to your discussion, rubbing the stone periodically to release the necessary energy.

Kindness—Charity—Service

There are days that I wonder if kindness and common courtesy have gone by the wayside. There are other times I wish that I (or someone else) had a better awareness of the need for charity and service in our own community. Let's face it, we've been part of a "me" generation for *more* than a generation! Our lives have become so hectic that the little niceties often get overlooked. This is a shame, but it's a situation to which a little well-applied magick might provide some remedies. These aren't quick fixes—one must be mindful to remember that true change begins within—but rather helpmates to the process of remembering these important considerations.

* Time your spells for when it's warm outside (physical warmth symbolizes the emotional warmth you're trying to achieve). Monday is also a good day because the moon is associated with feelings.

* Add aromatics such as elderflower or rose, but keep it light—kindness should not overwhelm!

* Use white or orange candles. White represents pure intentions, while orange is the harvest, the return of good karma.

* Include other potential components and symbols that represent benevolence and thoughtfulness to you (flowers seem to be popular).

This spell requires a large bowl into which you can place a taper candle securely. Also, pick out a bill (any denomination) that will act as "seed" money and put it in the bowl. Light the candle every day when you come in the door from an outing and toss your spare change into the bowl. If you have an area of your life that needs a little more charity, kindness, or service, think of it during this process. Blow out the candle when you're done focusing on those goals. Continue this process every day until the bowl is full.

Now, this is the important part. When the bowl is full you MUST give that money (all *but* the seed bill) to someone in need or a charity of your choice. The idea here is to inspire charity and service by doing the same yourself. If the candle grows low at any time, light a new one from the flame of the first and replace it. Keep the remnant wax to remelt for any magick that has a giving focus. (If you'd like a ready-made model to use for this spell, you can order them at *www.loresinger.com.*)

Those who serve, likewise, need service. The tragic reality of our community is that many of our elders and teachers are burning out. Use your candlelit spells to give them a little more energy and honor their contributions.

To begin, pick out a handful of teachers who have touched your life deeply. Next, choose a candle to represent them, carving their initials into the wax. Put the candles into holders and then place them somewhere special (an altar is ideal). Every month, on the night of the full moon, light the candles and direct the energy of that time to the person's spirit represented by that flame. Leave the candles burning for three hours to charge body, mind, and spirit equally. Do this for an entire year, replacing the candles as necessary, then perhaps drop those people a little letter sharing your thoughtfulness with them along with a little saved wax that they can use as an amulet or charm.

Kinship

The word kinship means "of the same nature or mind." True kinship has very little to do with blood ties and more to do with how we feel toward special people in our lives. I know that I have friends who are truly "kin" in heart and spirit. We share certain bonds that were built with tenacity and time. And while one cannot stop the ongoing maintenance it takes to keep kinship alive between two or more people, you can enact candlelight spells, meditations, and rituals to support your ties to one another. This support does not come in the form of constraint, but rather to keep the spiritual lines of communication open and vital.

- ※ Time your spells for when the sun is shining (it implies blessings), during a waxing moon, or during the months of June and July (most popular for reunions and weddings).
- ※ Add aromatics such as rosemary (for remembrance), lemon (friendship), orchid (love), and nutmeg (fidelity).
- ※ Use pink candles for gentle love.
- ※ Include other potential components and symbols such as trees (a family tree in particular), coats of arms, knots or rings, and jade (a stone that inspires good feelings between people).

Enact this mini-ritual on special occasions such as holidays, anniversaries, and birthdays when the members of your group or family cannot get together to celebrate. It will require a little planning to pull this off, however. First, you'll need to send a special candle to every person who wants to participate. These should all match in color, aroma, etc., and bear a mark that somehow represents the whole group.

Next, you need to choose a date and time when you can all work (remember to consider time differences in your planning). On the appointed day and hour, go to a window and set up your candle. Look toward the horizon and think of your friends or family who are also doing the same. Light the candle and softly chant:

"Though we are apart—we are of one heart.
Our spirits and minds, this magick binds.
Across the land, our love we send.
By this candle's light—our souls unite!"

Continue repeating the chant for about 15 minutes (or for whatever time you've agreed upon). When you stop, close your eyes and let hugs from near and far surround you astrally. Accept the warmth extended by others, and rejoice in it.

During this activity, you'll be making a special candle for someone who is going away (be it to college, moving to a new home, etc.). You'll need some pink candle wax and two jade stones (small pieces are best). You also need some type of candle mold. You can get these inexpensively at most hobby and craft shops.

Wait until the second night of the full moon to prepare this candle. Melt the wax over a low flame, and, if you wish, add some aromatics that will remind that person of you or home. Pour a little of the melted wax in the bottom and let it cool slightly. Place the two stones together (touching each other) into that wax, saying:

"My heart to your heart—never apart
When you feel lonely—know you're near to me
Then when this candle burns, my love will return!"

Pour in the remaining wax, place the wick, and let it cool. When you unmold the candle, wrap it in a soft cloth with a copy of the above incantation so the person understands how to use it.

❧ ❧ ❧

This mini-ritual strengthens the sense of kinship in a group. For it, each person must bring a candle to the gathering marked in a manner that's easily recognizable. Additionally, the person coordinating the event should bring some white, yellow, and blue ribbon (the colors of peace, communication, and joy, respectively) braided together. The altar is empty but for each person's candle. In turn around the Circle, everyone should light their candle and state their feelings toward the whole (also any wishes and goals). When everyone is done, the coordinator (often a priest or priestess) may blow out the candles and bind them with the ribbon. These should be stored safely away to protect the group's unity. If someone leaves the group in the future, the bundle is opened and the individual candle retrieved out of it, then resecured.

Learning (Knowledge/Understanding)

Curiosity is the wick in the candle of learning.
—William A. Ward

Linguistically, knowledge is a wonderful word. It has a depth of definition ranging from perceiving with sincerity, and distinguishing and recognizing, to the Biblical sense of having intimate relations. Learning simply means to gain that knowledge—that awareness and insight that we can apply readily in our lives.

Learning and understanding certainly doesn't end when one graduates from school. Life is an ongoing classroom, and I don't know about anyone else but my learning curve has been challenged a lot by the ongoing technical growth and other socioeconomic transformations in our society. Quite honestly, I find it hard to keep up. When I do, I employ one of these spells or an adaptation to give me a proverbial brain boost.

- ❃ Time your spells for when the moon is in Scorpio, Leo, or Taurus, Sundays, and bright days (for example, the "light" of understanding).
- ❃ Add aromatics such as rosemary for memory retention, or vanilla, marjoram, and mint for the conscious mind.
- ❃ Use yellow candles (to represent the Air Element, which governs our "thinking" self).
- ❃ Include other potential components and symbols such as glasses, notebooks, walnuts, amethyst, coral, and fluorite, all of which stress successful learning and the effective applications of one's skills.

To make this learning charm, gather a yellow candle, an aromatic of your choice, a small piece of paper (2 x 4 is good), and your favorite pen. Light the candle and take a few minutes to center yourself. Focus on your intention (especially the topic of which you hope to comprehend more). Write the name of that topic on the paper you when you feel your intention fully directed. Pick up the paper and speak the word thereon so that your breath falls across the sheet (breath gives life to energy). Finally, fold it in half, in half again, and in half again (three times all told), sealing it with wax as you might a letter. Keep this inside your notebook or other study materials.

꙰ ꧁ ꧂ ꙰

Make yourself a special learning/understanding candle. For this, you'll need wax, a wick, aromatics of your choice, some crushed coral, and a candle mold. You can get nearly everything you need at a good hobby shop, and coral can be crushed fairly easily using a rock to break it into smaller pieces (wrap it in a cloth first so you don't loose any).

Melt the wax, adding the aromatic chosen. Pour a little of this into the bottom of the mold, sprinkling coral into the foundation as you say:

"The coral of wisdom, to my mind beacons
As the light of the candle shines,
So, too, my understanding awakens.
When ever this candle burns,
Improve my ability to learn!"

Pour in the remaining wax and add the wick. After you release the candle from its mold light the candle any time you're sitting down to study or learning something new, and keep it burning nearby.

Note: You can save a little time by pouring the melted wax into a glass container that then becomes a self-enclosed housing for the candle (meaning you won't need a holder).

Love

Of all the requests I get for help with spellcasting, Love Magick ranks the highest. I find this worrisome in one respect: Love should not be manipulated. When it is, the meaning is lost. Therefore, when I teach people love spells I preface it by asking them to think long and hard about what they want, what they need, and how to achieve those goals without manipulation (bearing in mind that what we *think* we need and what we truly need are often two different things). I submit the same advice to you along with one other thought: release your Love Magick to the world without necessarily focusing it on ONE person. When love comes back to you, in any form, it is a blessing. Try not to put such a powerful and positive force into a preconceived box. You'll find your magick will respond in kind and find interesting ways to bring and keep love in your life.

❄ Time your spells for the full moon (a very romantic time). Alternatively, when the moon is in Aquarius or during the month of June.

❄ Add aromatics such as rose, apple, basil, cinnamon, lavender, lemon, orange, pine, and vanilla, all of which have long associations with love.

❄ Use pink or red candles (the darker the color, the deeper the level of intent).

❄ Include other potential components and symbols such as a heart or knots. Crystals such as amethyst (peaceful love), amber, jade, lapis, and moonstone. Also, mead has long been considered a love/fertility philter (which is why it was a traditional honeymoon gift).

Pick out a candle of the right color for your intention. Place a pin in the middle of the candle focusing on your significant other. Light the candle saying:

"As this candle burns
Let my love be returned.
If it be for the best
Then pray heed, my heart's request."

Note: This incantation provides a loophole: "If it be for the best." Should your relationship be an unhealthy one, this incantation insures that your magick won't feed the negativity. Let the candle burn until the pin falls out. You may use the remaining candle in other love spells.

This spell focuses on bringing new love into your life. A good time for it is during the Spring when Earth, itself, is blossoming with hope. Pick out one candle to represent yourself. Surround it with eight other pink or red candles (again chosen for the intensity of the relationship desired).

This spell takes place over eight days, and I suggest starting as the moon waxes out of the dark phase.

Pick out a time that you can work, undisturbed, every night at the same time. Begin by lighting one candle and speaking into the flame of your wishes. On night two, move the exterior candles a little closer to the candle that represents you and repeat this process with *two* candles. Continue in this manner until on the eighth night the eight candles are nearly touching the self candle. Let all naturally burn out releasing your wishes to the universe.

⚜ ⚜ ⚜

If you want to improve a relationship (specifically the level of trust) try this spell along with your mundane efforts. Begin with three candles (one to represent you, one for your mate, and one for your relationship as a whole), and three rose quartz crystals. Surround these with a combination of pink and green candles (green is for growth and health). If possible, you should enact this spell with your mate (or, minimally, ensure their goals for your relationship are the same as yours).

Begin the spell at dawn each day, for three days. On day one, light your candle, look at your mate, and share all that's in your heart and spirit. Put aside trivial issues, and really focus on all the goodness you have, and all that you hope will come. On day two, light your candle, your mate lights his or her candle, and then shares their joys, hopes, and dreams. Finally, on day three, you each light your personal candle. Then, from those two flames, both ignite the relationship candle, repeating together:

"In trust and love, blessed from above
As we carry this stone, our love to hone
In unity and harmony, we declare this spell is free!"

Leave the candles to burn and spend some quality time together. Each of you should always carry one of the three crystals with you, leaving the last one on your altar to represent your united minds and hearts.

Luck

I am willing to bet that if you randomly walk up to 10 strangers, and ask them if they wish they had more luck, the answer would be a resounding YES. Almost everyone I know (even those who *are* a little lucky) can certainly use a little more good fortune. When you feel like you've been plagued with ongoing red tape and barriers, when everything seems to be breaking or going wrong, or when you just would appreciate a lucky turn to put a smile on your face, try these spells:

The only *caution* I have is that luck is a persnickety creature and often manifests in an odd form. For example, I was working magick for luck in job-hunting that resulted in networking leads. This was great but it created a ton of work, too! That's the way the Universe prefers to manifest, by bringing us the kind of luck no one can take away because we've helped create it with honest efforts.

❄ Time your spells for when the sun is shining (or Sundays), when the moon is in Pisces, and Spring mornings.

❄ Add aromatics such as allspice, basil, heather, and nasturtium, all of which have fortunate energies.

❄ Use your lucky color for the candle's hue.

❄ Include other potential components and symbols of luck such as dice and coins; edibles such as beans, corn, red rice, and kiwi; and stones such as jade, moonstone, tin, and carnelian.

This spell requires a candle, some organic marigold petals, and water. To prepare, you'll need to simmer the marigolds in warm water until you get a tea-like infusion (one handful of marigold petals to one cup of water is fine). Add a little sugar to the tea if you wish, to emphasize sweet fortune.

Next, light the candle with the cup of marigold tea nearby, saying:

> *"As the light of hope shines,*
> *May good fortune be mine.*
> *And as I internalize this lucky tea,*
> *All good things shall come to me!"*

Drink the tea completely, accepting its energy. Leave the candle (in a safe place) to burn itself out.

Find a large bay leaf on which you write the word luck. Take a candle in your lucky color and light it. Focus on your intention to bring good fortune to one specific area of your life. Light the bay leaf from the candle and place it in a fire-safe container to burn. As it releases smoke, use your hand to move the smoke upward toward the heavens saying:

> *"Higher and higher, my wish from the fire:*
> *Luck be kind, luck come quick.*
> *Luck released from this candle's wick!"*

Once the bay leaf has burned completely out, take the remaining ashes outside and release them to the winds so that your wish is scattered to the Four Corners of creation. Blow out the candle and use it for other luck spells.

When you're having a streak of unusually bad luck, this spell may help break that negativity: Wait until the moon is waning (you want to banish the bad fortune). Light a black candle and walk through the entire house counter clockwise. Stop in each room and recite an incantation such as:

"Into the darkness, away from light
All ill will retreats, all bad fortune takes flight
Only goodness abounds, good luck surrounds."

Repeat this in every room of the house and then break the black candle to symbolically "break" the hold of bad luck.

Magickal Aptitude (Spirituality)

Magick is a methodology; spirituality is an ideology. In the context of this book, I have typically kept magick and spirituality appearing as a cooperative effort because that is how it should be. I realize there are some readers who simply practice the art of magick without any particular ideology or philosophy behind it—it's simply a tool. Because that's not how I live my life, I can't teach that way!

I believe that the spirit or art that does not grow and reach beyond it's present state will wither and die as surely as a plant that doesn't reach out with roots for water. Allowing our magick to grow with personal and planetary transformations is essential. With that in mind, these candle spells endeavor to achieve a harmony of art and idea, and then an empowering of that partnership so you can grow and advance on your Path. They can also be used as a way of safeguarding yourself against ill-intended magicks.

* Time your spells for when the moon is full or midnight (the Witching Hour), or when the moon is in Pisces.
* Add aromatics such as carnation (power), lilac, sandalwood (magickal aptitude and psychism), and lotus (spirituality).
* Use a purple candle (for spiritual pursuits and wisdom) or a white candle (to represent the human spirit).

❋ Include other potential components and symbols such as a bell, book, keys, any magickal tools (such as a wand or athame), and rowan or willow wood.

There is an old European folk belief that a Witch's power resides in their hair. Building on this concept, take three strands of your hair and braid them together saying:

> *"Three by one, the spell is begun.*
> *Three by two, the power is true.*
> *Three by three, magick in me!"*

Tie this braid around your chosen candle. Then the next time you need to increase the energy of a spell, light it and recite the incantation three times before enacting your spell or ritual. Leave the candle burning while you work.

⁂

This is a little household charm that's an adaptation of the anti-magick Witch Bottles people use to keep malevolent spells away. To begin, you'll need a flat-bottomed container into which you secure a black candle (to absorb negativity). Around the candle, place pieces of old, broken glass, rusted nails or anything else sharp, gnarly, and reflective (to entangle or turn negative energy). There doesn't need to be a lot of these things, just enough so that the bottom of the container is covered. Leave this item near your hearth (a fireplace or stove), and light it when you feel a spell or ritual has raised energy against you (or when you feel psychically attacked).

⁂

This spell acts as a way of creating fast sacred space to amplify your magick. For it you need four candles—one red, one blue, one brown or green, one yellow. Bless these candles, saying:

"I charge you each, candles four—guard well, safeguard
magick's door.
As watchtowers and guides pure,
all unwanted influences deter,
And with this flame I now ignite,
the power in this spell takes to flight!"

Put these candles as close as possible to the Four directional Quarters in your home or magickal workroom. Light them just before enacting any magick for which you'd like both a sacred space and an energy boost. You can use the same incantation to "turn on" their energy should you wish, or use another invocation of your own for the Elements.

Meditation

"The best candle is understanding."
—Welsh Proverb

Plenty of people have trouble meditating. If you fall into this category, don't feel bad. It's normal for the human mind to want to juggle multiple concepts and tasks at the same time. However, the goal of meditation is different—namely to focus in on one area, one problem, or to simply release yourself from thinking long enough to destress. Meditation can bring down your blood pressure! For the purpose of this section, we'll examine both a candlelight meditation and a spell, both of which are aimed at improving the overall meditation experience so that you get the desired results.

❋ Time your spells for dusk or evening
  (darkness seems to improve the affect for
  most people), and during the full moon (for
  improved insight).

❋ Add aromatics such as sandalwood, lotus,
  and sweetgrass, all of which are used to

create a highly-charged atmosphere for
internal workings.

✳ Use a blue or white candle.

✳ Include other potential components and
symbols such as amethyst, fluorite, and silver
(all of which accent the meditative process).
Also, consider chimes or a drumbeat to help
center your mind and thoughts.

For this activity, you'll need a small drum or any object that can act as a drum (such as a hollow log or an
overturned potted bowl) and a blue candle. Think about
the things in your life that require some serious contem-
plation. Pick out one topic for this meditation and carve a
symbol (or a words) of that topic into the candle. Focus
wholly on your intent to broaden your perspectives on that
topic (or whatever other insights you need).

Next, light the candle. Put your hands, palms down,
on the drum's surface and breath deeply. Listen closely
for the sound of your heartbeat. Mirror that rhythm on
the drum, focusing on both the sound and your intention.
Once the beat becomes natural, allow images of the topic
at hand to form in your mind. Don't try to hold them or
force them. You will remember them afterward, so just let
go and allow mind, heart, and spirit to work cooperatively.

When the images cease, or you start loosing your ability
to concentrate, stop the drumming and make notes of your
experience. Read them over once or twice while the candle
still burns so it can illuminate your understanding. Blow out
the candle and keep it for other meditative moments.

❧ ⚬⚬⚬ ❧

In Eastern traditions, meditation need not be something that's still. There are walking meditations and even

dancing meditations. We live in a highly-mobile society, so this idea holds a lot of merit. The idea behind this bit of magick is to make yourself a charm for carrying during your moving meditations:

Begin with a candle, some lotus oil, and a crystal of your choice. Light the candle. Hold the stone in your weak hand while dabbing it with a bit of oil using your strong hand. Rub this in as if you're using the crystal as a worry stone, but be focused on your desire for the stone to become a cue for moving meditations. If you wish, add an incantation such as:

"Focus be born, distraction abate;
Help me as I meditate."

Place a drop or two of wax on the stone and wrap it in a soft cloth. Carry this with you when you take walks or try other forms of moving meditation. If you can touch the stone periodically (especially when you feel distracted), it improves the results.

Memory

We have a saying in my house: "If it's not written down, it does not exist." This has come about due to my propensity for writing lists and notes and leaving them everywhere so I remember everything that needs to be done. Without them, I fear my life would fall into chaos. But what about the times that there are no papers, or strings to tie around your finger? Or the times when you need to be certain of remembering important things without any prop or prompting (such as your lines for a wedding ritual or the date of your anniversary)? The goal behind candlelight memory spells and charms is one of shining a light into the corners of your mind where that information's stored (but where it also sometimes seems to hide, out of reach).

※ Time your spells for daylight hours (if trying to remember "conscious mind" items, or during moonlight for more esoteric memorization), or when the moon is in Aries.

※ Add aromatics such as rosemary, apple, vanilla, and coffee, all of which strengthen the mind.

※ Use a yellow candle.

※ Include other potential components and symbols such as mustard seed, quartz crystals (for clarity), a memory chip from a computer, or knots (to hold the learning, rather than lose it).

I like to combine memory spells with something portable simply because I usually need to remember something when I do NOT have access to a fast reference. The two spells I'm sharing here are constructed with that kind of situation in mind (rather like magickally tying a string around your finger.

This first one requires a quartz crystal and a candle. Take the quartz outside under the bright sunshine to absorb the energy. In a nearby area, light the candle. Recite all the information or tasks that you need to remember into the crystal and the flame of the candle. When you're done doing this, drop a bit of the candle wax on the crystal, saying:

> *"As sure as wax from this flame*
> *Remembrance I claim*
> *When held to my brain*
> *The memories retain*
> *When held to my heart*
> *Your information impart!"*

Following the pattern of the spell, hold the crystal to your forehead and recite your list or information again, then tuck it in your pocket. Put the crystal to your heart when you sense you're forgetting something.

The second spell begins as the first, but this time you need a length of yellow ribbon or yarn and a candle. Light the candle and look over the materials you need to remember by the warmth of its light. Next, take up the length of ribbon or yarn, and tie pieces of information into it by speaking into the strand what you need to remember, then adding:

"Bound within, the spell beings
When unwound, memory abounds!"

Repeat this process all the way down the length of the yarn or ribbon. You can make this as long or short as you want, but don't try to cram too much information into each knot. Just like a mundane knot, it will only house so much. Typically, I put one factoid or chore in each knot. Taking this one step further, I sometimes color code the knots using a marker (brown for a household chore, yellow for a birthday, etc.). That way, when I realize I can't remember, I can undo the knot that releases the correct information.

An alternative to this would be to make a general memory Witch's ladder (the length of knots is called that by tradition). Use the very same incantation when tying the knots, but don't focus on any specific type of information. Dab these knots with some rosemary oil and open one at a time as needed. Just do not open the last knot. When the strand gets down to one, recharge it with fresh magick and new knots.

Money

Just as with health, happiness, and luck, money is one of those things that we both need, and of which we often wish we had more. My mother told me that money doesn't buy happiness, but it makes it a lot easier! I agree. While there's a difference between greed and need, I see no reason not to utilize magick to help us prosper so that we can focus a little more time on family, friends, and our spiritual lives.

As with other touchy ethical issues, the results from Money Magick can be quite surprising. Typically when I ask for money, I am given extra work through which to make that money. I see this in other people's lives too—almost as a Universal means of checks and balances that keeps us honest! So be prepared to roll up your sleeves.

- ❋ Time your spells for when the moon is in Aquarius or Pisces, a blue moon, Sundays, New Year's, or any day in Spring (for growth oriented energy).
- ❋ Add aromatics such as cedar, dill, vetiver, almond, basil, cinnamon, orange, nutmeg, and woodruff.
- ❋ Use green, silver, or gold candles (green for paper money, silver for smaller amounts, and gold for larger amounts).
- ❋ Include other appropriate components and symbols such as a dollar sign, rice, moss agate, alfalfa, piggy banks, and your wallet.

Collect a wide-based candle in the color of your choice, a silver or gold coin (preferably one minted in the year of your birth), and some high quality olive oil (an old Italian charm for prosperity). Perform the actual working during the waxing to full moon for growth-oriented energies.

Begin by warming the bottom of your candle just enough to press the coin into it (you want money at the foundation of the candle's energy). When that's secure, dress the candle in olive oil, moving clockwise with your fingers upward from the base of the candle. Focus wholly on your intent to improve the overall flow of money in your home.

Next, at dawn each morning, light the candle, saying:

"As the candle glows
And wax flows
Let money grow."

Continue until the moon is in the second day of fullness then retain the candle for the following month. If you wish, keep your wallet or checkbook nearby when enacting the spell and carry a bit of the wax remnants as a money charm.

❦ ❧

This is a good spell to enact on New Year's, but it can be done any time when family and friends are present. Have everyone contribute some loose change to a clear container. Put this on a table. Next, take one candle for each person present and surround the jar completely. Those who wish to participate should light their own candle and take *one* coin from the jar to leave near their personal taper. As they remove their coin, they should think of the amount of money they truly need (not want, but really need). Once everyone has done this, join hands and chant together:

"Restrictions decrease.
Money increase.
In the light of the flame,
Our wishes we claim."

Continue to repeat this until your voices raise and naturally crescendo. At this point break hands and raise them upward to send the magick on its way. Each person keeps his or her coin and candle (the coin as a money charm, and the candle for money magick at home). The rest of the jar should be used for a charitable purpose.

Movement

Movement is tied in with the course and process of change. It is not simply about getting from here to there, but about both literal and figurative transformation that provides some kind of progress in a specific direction. So, when you feel like you're spinning your wheels and seek a spiritual tow truck, these candle spells and charms offer that kind of option. They will also help you when you're facing a choice or challenge and feel frozen in your tracks because of its difficulty.

* Time your spells for right after the dark moon (when everything starts moving forward again) or the season of Spring.

* Add energetic aromatics such as ginger, carnation, vanilla, marigold, or thyme.

* Use a candle whose color represents the area of your life that seems to be stagnating or moving too slowly.

* Include other potential components and symbols that have some type of action to them such as kinetic toys, pinwheels, etc. You want to visually put the magick into motion to mirror your intention.

For this spell, you'll need a candle into which you've carved an emblem of the area of your life where the need exists. You also need a children's pinwheel, a small paint-brush, and a magic marker. Write a word that describes your need on each of the pinwheel's sections. Lay it aside.

Next, melt the candle in a non-aluminum pan until the carved emblem disappears. Use the paintbrush to apply a very light coating of the wax over the word you've written on the pinwheel as you say:

"Hear my prayer, hear my request
By my will, this spell manifests
Change, unfold—the powers behoove
With life's breath, things start to move!"

Now, focus wholly on your need and blow on the pin-wheel to put it into motion. If you can leave this outside to let the winds help spiral the energy, all the better. Save your wax for any type of spell that requires a little mani-festing energy.

⁓⁓⁓

This spell is designed to take place over the span of at least a week (longer if necessary). First, you need to get a good amount of self-enclosed candles (the large ones such as the ones you can get at Christian stores). If possible, get them in rainbow colors, arranging them from red to purple, so that the color of the candle progresses forward, similar to how you want other things to move forward.

Starting on the first day of a waxing moon, light the candle saying:

"The first light burns and shall not go out.
It is my wish, my heart's desire."

This candle should remain burning continually until the next night. At that time, you can use a twig or a long-handled match to light the second candle from the flame of the first. (If you need to replace any candles during this process because they give out, always light the re-placement from the original to illustrate the continua-tion of energy.) As you light the second candle, say:

"The first light burns, it is my wish—my heart's desire
The second light burns, supporting the first,
creating light in the darkness."

Continue this process following the same pattern, repeating this incantation to the line that corresponds with the day:

"The first light burns,
it is my wish—my heart's desire (day one).
The second light burns true, supporting the first,
bringing light to the darkness (day two).
The third light burns in me,
giving me the hope and power to keep trying (day 3).
The fourth light burns
guiding energy toward my goal (day 4).
The fifth light burns,
overcoming any blockages (day 5).
The sixth light burns,
and the wheel of time turns (day 6).
The seventh light shines,
what I wish is mine!"

Let these burn out naturally after the seventh candle.

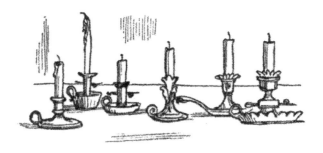

Networking

*"There are two ways of spreading light: To be the candle or
the mirror that reflects it."*

—Edith Wharton

Word of mouth is still the best way to go about getting
good information from those who have "been there and done
that." Among Neo-Pagans, networking has been elevated
to a new art. We've depended on it heavily for a great deal
of things, ranging from finding teachers to locating a decent
organic herbal shop. What happens, however, when your
normal web-weaving contacts come up empty handed?
That's the ideal time to pull out a little magick.

* Time your spells for dusk (networking
  requires a balance of rational and intuitive
  thought, and dusk often allows for both
  sunlight and moonlight at the same time).
  Alternatively, wait until the moon is in
  Virgo to encourage fruitful alliances.

* Add aromatics such as lemon (for
  networking with friends), heather (for a
  little luck), and ginger (for success).

* Use a white candle (because you never
  know what form your networking contacts
  may take).

* Include other potential components and
  symbols such as webs (or string), carnelian
  or beryl (for effective communication),
  eastern winds (to carry your missives), and
  a telephone.

This activity uses a candle and string as a type of pendulum (specifically when you're trying to find contacts in

an area of which you have a map). Begin by securing the candle with a length of string that will allow you to hold the candle upside down over the map with your elbow securely on the table outside the outer edge of the map. Be thinking about your networking questions as you tie the knot in place, saying:

*"A web to weave, a_____to find
In wax now leave a trail behind!"*

Fill in the blank with what you're looking for (such as a coven, a new age store, etc.) If you find that the thread slips off the candle, you can use some melted wax from a second one to hold it sure. Now, light the candle and suspend it carefully about 5 inches above the surface of the map. Steady the unlit end with your other hand. Again, focus on your question and repeat the incantation eight times, slowly. Try not to look directly at the map so you don't accidentally skew this divination effort (your hand will often follow eye movement). When you're done, blow out the candle and see what patterns or areas the wax dripped upon.

This spell is similar to the first, but this time you'll need about 2 feet of cotton thread (any color) a picture of a spider web, and your candle. Put the image of the web under the candle (the foundation for the magick) on a fire-safe surface. Now, lay the candle at the center point of the cotton thread and crisscross the thread upward from the bottom of the candle, tying a knot at each cross point saying:

*"Grandmother spider, teacher of words,
Weave your web in my life, let my prayer be heard,
One to one, one to three, exponentially out from me,
Thread to thread, mind to mind, help me with
a_____to find."*

Set the candle up right on the image and light it.

Note: You can fill in the blank with the same networking need at each knot, or different needs. When the candle burns the knot open, it releases the magick.

Oaths (Promises)

An oath or vow is a kind of magick unto itself. Those of a metaphysical persuasion, however, like to bring a more ritualistic overtone to such moments and support our promises with a spiritual commitment too. This comes from the understanding that a promise is not simply words—it's intention, which is also at the heart of magick. No matter how good our intentions may be, some promises are very hard to keep, so supporting them with a little extra energy makes sense.

- Time your spells for when the moon is in Libra (for equity), a Tuesday (if making a legal commitment), or Friday (for relationship promises).
- Add aromatics such as lilac for harmony, magnolia (peace and devotion), and myrrh (protection).
- Use a white candle for pure motivations.
- Include other potential components and symbols, such as bluebell or eyebright (to determine honest intent), agate (for blessing the promise), cups, and knots.

This activity is designed specifically for the promise made between a couple, either for an engagement, handfasting, wedding, or similar commitment. For it you'll need about 4 feet of deep red, pink, and white yarn, some rose oil, and a white candle. Carve a heart or other symbol of your promise into the candle. Light it, and sit nearby as you braid the yarn and chant:

> *"Two hearts, true hearts from us both*
> *Braided three by three, let us honor our oath!"*

When the braid is completed, wax both ends so it doesn't come undone, then blow out the candle. There are several ways you can use this strand at this point. It can become the handfasting "cloth" for binding the couple's hands at the end of the ritual, or you could wrap the strand around the candle and store them in a safe place to protect the commitment made.

❧ ❧ ❧

This charm is for people who find they sometimes have trouble fulfilling the commitments they make. Begin with a candle, two eye agates, a 3 x 3 cloth, and a string. Light the candle and focus on your intent to be more dependable (or minimally not to overextend yourself). Put the two eye agates in the center of the cloth, saying:

> *"Eyes of spirit, eyes of mind,*
> *In this pouch my magick bind.*
> *A promise to keep, a promise once made,*
> *From my mind it never fades."*

Drip a little candle wax into the center of the cloth, then bundle it with the string. Keep this with you whenever you're juggling a lot of different responsibilities.

Opportunity

No one wants to be in the middle of the desert when their ship finally comes in. Then again, I tend to be away from home when opportunity finally knocks. To avoid these types of situations and open up more opportunity in all areas of your life, try these candle spells and see what kind of chances come your way.

* Time your spells for dawn, Spring (the time of openings and awakenings), during the waxing to full moon, or when the moon is in Taurus.
* Add aromatics such as apple, nutmeg, and vanilla.
* Use a candle whose color represents the area of your life in which the opportunity is needed (for work you might use brown or green to stress the Earth Element, for example).
* Include other potential components and symbols such as doors, keys, windows, bridges, and can openers (all of which imply some type of opening or movement).

This activity requires an outdoor container such as a lantern to house your chosen candles (so you can still burn them if it rains). You'll also need seven candles, and an aromatic of your choice. Dab this lantern with an aromatic that best represents your goal, then carve an image of that goal into the wax on each candle. During the next week, take one candle outside your house each morning at dawn and light it, saying:

"As the sun brings a new day, so too open the way
Hear my prayer and to me bring many more openings!"

Leave the candle to burn while you go about your tasks. Bring it in at dusk. Repeat over the full seven days, each day with a fresh candle. Keep your eyes and ears open for opportunity's knock.

From the wax in the last activity and an old key, you can make yourself a portable opportunity charm. Warm the wax by rubbing it between your hands so it gets soft enough to shape around the key. As you form it to the key, try chanting something such as:

"Magick saturate this little key,
Bring to me opportunity!"

Keep repeating the phrase until the key is enclosed in the wax then carry it with you regularly. Note: If you're ever in a situation where you need a very fast response, take the key out of the wax saying:

"Unlock the magick in my key,
By my will the spell is free!"

If you're wondering where an opportunity might lie and have a variety of possibilities, you can use candle drippings as a type of divination to help. To put this activity into a functional example, if you have several potential jobs for which to apply and want to limit your choices to the best ones, cut those ads from the paper or gather the business cards. Lay them out randomly on a piece of craft paper (face down).

Next, light a yellow candle (for communication and messages). Concentrate on your goal of choosing the right positions. Hold that candle in your strong hand, and without looking at the pieces of paper, mix them up with your free hand. Now, hold the candle over the surface (don't look down—you don't want to skew the reading) and repeat this incantation four times (an Earth number that correlates with "Job"-Oriented Magick). Obviously if your networking goal is different, change the number of repetitions.

"My efforts and focus, pray direct,
Let my choices be correct!"

Finally, look at the ads or cards that wax landed on and begin there.

Organization

Organization is not a four-letter word! Having everything in order has many advantages. In the Eastern system of feng shui (the art of placement), orderliness (over clutter) opens the flow of beneficial energy in any space. Similarly, in metaphysical traditions, organization provides a framework within which everything flows more smoothly. Unfortunately, maintaining a tidy composition or ordered methodology aren't personal traits that come easily or naturally to many people. And while you'll have to continue to make efforts on a mundane level to develop those aptitudes, there's no reason not to look for spiritual support, too.

⁂ Time your spells for noon (to emphasize rational orderly thought), Spring-cleaning time, when the moon is in Leo, or Sundays.

⁂ Add aromatics that strengthen the conscious mind such as rosemary, apple, and almond.

⁂ Use a gold or vibrant orange candle.

⁂ Include other potential components and symbols such as a note pad, palm organizer, a calculator, cleaning implements, or a filing cabinet. Also try fire-oriented stones (to put a fire under those projects) such as red agate and amber.

For this activity, all you'll need is a gold candle dabbed with a chosen aromatic and a little undisturbed time. Sit comfortably in front of the candle and light it. Breathe deeply and relax. Watch the candle long enough that you can see it clearly in your mind's eye, then close your eyes.

Next, visualize the flame of the candle growing larger until it surrounds you. Let this saturate your aura until the entire aura glows with a golden hue. If you can see the light like a patterned matrix (geometric) all the better— patterns represent order. When you feel yourself growing warm from this exercise, change your perspective slightly and imagine the area of your life that needs to be put in order. Surround it with the same patterned energy glow. Continue until you feel that energy fixed in place (this is hard to describe but you just "know" it's done).

Return to normal awareness then immediately take your candle into that area of your life, light it again, and get busy!

◦ ◌ ◦

This is a nice edible treat that you can prepare and eat in the light of your energized candle. Take one apple and slice it. Fry it lightly in butter and rosemary (go light on the rosemary). Stir the mix clockwise in the pan to work with "sun" energy, saying:

> *"Apple for wisdom, and spice for my mind,*
> *Within this food ordered magick combines!"*

Keep repeating the incantation while you cook. Then sit down with a lit candle and let the light of motivation shine on your food. Repeat the incantation silently in your mind while you consume the apple. Eating internalizes the energy you've created.

◦ ◌ ◦

This spell takes place over eight days. Start by putting any four candles you happen to have handy out on a surface so they're scattered. Each day at dawn, light the candles saying:

"Out of darkness comes light."

Then move the candles slightly so they're closer to being in a tidy line, saying:

"Out of chaos comes order."

Repeat this each day for the next three days (making sure the candles are lined up perfectly on the third day). If you can leave them in that area and light them only when you feel like you're getting disorganized, that's a great support system for the spell. If not, however, just let the candles burn naturally out.

Overcoming

"I continue to create because writing is a labor of love and also an act of defiance, a way to light a candle in a gale wind."

—Alice Childress

How many times have you felt like a situation was impossible? When you're faced with overwhelming odds, continual setbacks, a habit you can't seem to break, or the proverbial brick wall without a dent in sight, it's time to pull a little positive energy out of your Candle Magick kit. These spells are designed to give you a little more luck, personal fortitude, or the leg up when you need one most.

※ Time your spells for the waning to dark moon (so that obstacles shrink) or when the moon is in Aries (breaks down barriers) or in Scorpio (reverses negatives).

※ Add aromatics such borage (courage), bay (strength), and cinnamon (success).

※ Use a red colored candle (the Fire Element, which provides both burning energy and the capacity to destroy the obstacles).

❋ Include other potential components and
symbols such as items that loosen or open
(to likewise shake matters loose or create
new openings).

This activity begins with a candle of your choosing and
an image of the obstacle you face. Make sure the image is
something that combusts easily. For example, if you are
having trouble getting money, a picture of a dollar bill behind a door or in a box might work. You'll also want a
firesafe container where it can burn completely out. Light
your candle, and bring to mind the circumstances that frus-
trate while holding that image in your strong hand. Move
it to the flame saying:

"Barriers be broken, let the way be open."

When the image is caught fully, transfer it carefully to
the container, continuing to chant all the while it burns.
Watch as the obstacle is literally destroyed before your
eyes. When the flames are gone, blow out the candle and
bury the ashes so something positive can come of the mo-
mentary delays you've experienced. Keep the candle for
other similar spells (such as success and victory).

☙ ❦ ☙

This visualization uses a candle as a prop, but you can
certainly bring one into your private sacred space to improve the effect of the activity. Begin by getting comfortable in a chair (perhaps with your chosen candle in front
of you). Light the candle so you can keep a strong image
of how it looks in your mind's eye. Slowly release all ten-
sions and breath deeply.

When you feel centered, direct your mind to making
an imaginary paper wall before which you're standing astrally. On that wall are full images of everything that you

feel is presently holding you back. The left side of the paper are things in the past that you had to overcome. The images in front are present, and those to the right are still forming, but represent future obstacles.

Now, with faith and determination, take your mental candle, which came with you into the visualization, and burn the barrier away. When it is completely ash, take another deep breath and dissipate all that negativity completely to the wind. Return to normal awareness. Make notes of any interesting experiences that happened during (or after) the visualization.

Passion (Lust)

Sometimes you need to spark a fire. Other times you need to give it a little boost to burn brightly. Others still, when an interested party is a little too interested, you need to put that fire out! Whatever the case, when our amorous physical nature isn't cooperating the way we wish, it provides us with an opportunity to apply a little positive Candle Magick directly into our love lives.

* Time your spells for when the sun is shining (blessings), the full moon (a very romantic time), when the moon is in Scorpio, and on May Day.
* Add lustful aromatics such as cinnamon, hibiscus, mint, vanilla, and violet.
* Use deep red candles (to light the fires within).
* Include other potential components and symbols that are known to inspire passion. Among foods we find asparagus, banana, carrot, orange, fish, cucumbers, and eggs; For crystals, turn to those that have a vibrant red hue such as red agates and red jasper.

Rather than use a candle as the main component in this spell, let's consider using it as additional ambiance to set the mood for a mutually enjoyed passion potion. Begin with three cups of orange juice in a blender, about one-half of a banana, and a hint of vanilla extract. Whip this to frothy, saying:

"Round and round, burning desire,
Take our passions ever higher!"

Pour this into a cup (to unite your purpose with that of your mate) and drizzle with a little melted chocolate and sweet cream. Serve by candlelight, drink fully, and let Nature take her course.

❧ ❧ ❧ ❧ ❧

For this activity, you're going to make a special passion candle that you or your significant other can light as a signal when you're in the mood. Begin with red wax and a mold of your choice (I think something with sensual overtones would be apt, but a lot here depends on what kind of décor you can have around the house). In the base of the candle, place two red stones to represent each of you. Mingle whatever passionate aromatics you both like into the wax while it's cooling. Stir clockwise as you say:

"Two hearts—one flame
our passion reclaim."

Continue to whisper the incantation into the wax until it's ready to put into the mold. Use the incantation again each time you light the candle to unlock your magick.

❧ ❧ ❧ ❧ ❧

There are times when we want to cool down a relationship that's getting overheated. To accomplish this, take a candle that represents the overly interested person, dab it with his or her favorite aromatic, and carve their name into it. On each night from the waning to dark moon, light the candle, saying:

> *"Let _____'s passion grow gentle and calm,*
> *If it be his/her will, and it do no harm."*

This incantation does not manipulate the individual, but rather offers a cooling energy that they can accept or reject. However, I do suggest after completing the spell you place the candle in the freezer temporarily then go have a serious conversation with said individual, indicating how continued lustful behavior may negatively impact the relationship.

Passages, Rites of

> *"Out, out, brief candle! Life's but a walking shadow, a poor player That struts and frets his hour upon the stage And then is heard no more."*

—William Shakespeare, "Macbeth"

Nearly every important moment in human life has been commemorated somehow through rituals and mini-rituals. Rites of Passage are among the most important of these commemorations because they earmark our lives important transitions: birth, adulthood, eldership, and death. For the living, Rites of Passage provide an important opportunity to integrate our experiences and feelings. For the dead, they honor memories and send off the soul with good wishes on its journey.

As with holidays, the size of this book doesn't allow for extensive exploration of every Rite of Passage. I can, however, provide a list of suggestions on utilizing candles and aromatics for several. To this basic foundation, add your knowledge of the individual for whom the ritual is being performed. Talk to them about what they want, about what would be meaningful and memorable. Get friends and family involved. Surround the sacred space with love and thoughtfulness and you won't go wrong!

- **Birth:** While we enter this life with our past lives imprinted on our spirit, the newborn child is pure. A white candle, therefore, is appropriate. In terms of aromatics, please be careful. Some newborns can have negative reactions to aromas, so keep them light. I suggest simmering potpourri blend of lily of the valley and other white flowers to represent innocence.

- **Adulthood:** Because the child is about to take on an adult role in your household (and possibly at your Circle) let he or she pick out the candles and aromatics the child prefers. Ask them to think about the significance of each and share it with you so that meaning can be integrated into the words of the ritual. In terms of timing, many young women partake of this ritual when they have their first menses. Young men can be gauged by their behavior, but typically the ritual takes place between the age of 13 and 18, with the average being at age 16.

- **First home away from home:** Typically during college years, this is an excellent time to make a house candle that will represent the spirit of a new home, and encourage joy and peace within. The person living in the new house should make the candle (the color being their choice), but if they wish, they can form it from remnants of the candles of family and friends to inspire warm feelings.

- **Wedding or Handfasting:** This is a very real Rite of Passage that implies a unity of heart and spirit. One of the most common types of candle symbolism used at these rituals is that of two candles lighting one central candle to honor that oneness. Another lovely addition to late afternoon weddings, are candlelit processional areas, to illuminate the way toward a new life together.

❈ **Eldership:** When I think of the strongly grounded characteristics of an elder the first color that comes to mind is brown such as the color of soil that's accepted the sun and rain and been enriched. For aromatics, ask if the person has a god or goddess that they follow, then apply aromatics that honor that Deity.

❈ **Death:** Rites of Passage for the dead are designed to help the soul's transition and to provide a coping mechanism for those left behind. In this rite, I suggest having a white candle to represent Deity, and a candle whose color is chosen based on the deceased's favorite hue. Aromatics should be peaceful (such as lavender) or those that somehow celebrate that person's life (such as their favorite incense, perfume, or cologne).

As with all other candle-lighting efforts, don't overlook the importance of your intention as you place flame to wick in any of these rituals. Also, don't forget to trust your instincts and allow for those moments of inspired magick.

Peace (Quiet)

Our lives are literally inundated with sound. Honking horns, barking dogs, crying children, blaring radios—these things and many others intrude on our day nearly non-stop. So much is the case that it's no wonder we have trouble hearing the still, small voice of Spirit—S/he can't get a word in edgewise! This constant level of noise and commotion tends to leave people feeling out of sorts and restless (and often not knowing exactly why).

The beauty of metaphysics is that when a spell or ritual is enacted correctly, it can (and does) affect the temporal realm. In this case, you'll be using your magick to set up an astral barrier between you and the source of noise or disruptions so that some semblance of peace is restored.

* Time your spells for the waning moon so that noise or disruptions, dawn (for hope of a better start), or when the moon is in Libra.
* Add harmonious aromatics such as gardenia, lavender, myrtle, pennyroyal, and violet.
* Use a white candle (to signal a truce and pure intention).
* Include other potential components and symbols such as a white flag, willow wood (adaptive energy), amethyst (for self-control and improved serenity), or anything else that you associate with reclaiming tranquility.

To encourage peace in a specific situation or between yourself and another person, you can turn your candle into a poppet. For greatest effectiveness, I'd suggest a black candle to represent ire or negativity. From the last night of the full moon until the dark moon, light the candle saying:

"Hostilities cease, I reclaim peace!"

Continue reciting the incantation for a few minutes while you direct all the negative energy associated with that situation into the candle. On the last night of this activity, let the wax burn completely out. After the wax cools break it into tiny pieces (likewise breaking up the energy stored within) and dispose of it properly.

This activity provides a magickal means to open the way for peace between people. In this case I'm going to suggest you use the energy of a waxing moon to draw more positive energy into the situation. Also put the candles in a somewhat sunny location while you're burning them (to balance the emotional self with more rational thought).

Begin with one candle for each person involved in the dispute. Place these around a white central candle to represent the Spirit of Peace and Understanding. Each day, move the candles slightly closer to each other, then light them from the Spirit candle, saying:

"We come together joined by the Light of Spirit,
We grow closer to understanding, illuminated by wisdom,
We reach for peace and renewal,
With the spark of honorable intent,
We seek healing in the glow of mutual respect.
So be it."

On the final night of working (which should be the second night of the full moon before it begins to shrink), let these burn out naturally, then make your calls or go for a visit. See what opportunities Spirit makes for reconciliation.

I don't know about the rest of you, but it seems every person that knows me waits until the worst possible moment to call, visit, or have a need. There are times when all of us want to be left undisturbed, be it for magick or a decent nap. With this in mind, this activity is meant to encourage calm and quiet.

Take a white candle into the room where you want to create the sphere of silence. Light it in the eastern part of that room and begin walking the entire perimeter (clockwise to draw silence, counterclockwise to banish noise), visualizing the glow of the candle extending outward to the walls.

This wash of light covers the windows, doors, ceiling, air ducts, electrical outlets...everything in sight like a huge glowing bubble. Take up a comfortable spot in the center of that bubble and remain as long as your wish. Note, however, that if the candle goes out, the energy field dissipates fairly quickly.

Power

Has the spark in your wand fizzled out? Do you feel like every ritual or spell has a damper on it and the energy goes nowhere? Ever get the sense that you have absolutely no power to transform a specific situation? Each of these examples is a perfect reason to pull out come candlepower!

* Time your spells for Summer (esp. Summer Solstice), the full moon (for both rational and intuitive power), Tuesdays (strength), when the moon is in Scorpio (fiery energy), or when the overall ambient temperature outside is slowly rising.
* Add aromatics such as chrysanthemum, carnation, and ginger.
* Use red candles (or bright purple for power balanced with wisdom).
* Include other potential components and symbols such as batteries, a bell (to center the energy), hair (a Witch's power was said to reside here), and a wand or athame (both used to direct magickal energy/power).

This is a generalized power ritual that you can use to saturate yourself or any item you wish with energy. For best results, I suggest enacting it at dawn on Summer Solstice. The ritual requires a candle (or as many candles as you wish—this is a Fire festival) and four flowering seeds.

Begin by finding a spot where you can easily see the sunrise and where you have a flat surface on which to rest the candle. While you're waiting for the sun to rise, toss the seeds toward the Four Directions (one each), saying:

"Guardian of the East, empower my communications.
Guardian of the South, energize my conscious mind.
Guardian of the West, spark my emotions and psychic self.
Guardian of the North, illuminate my foundations."

Now, wait until you see the very first glimmers peeking across the horizon. Welcome them as you light the candle, saying:

"Sun reaching over the heights,
Fill me with power and light."

Spend as much time here as you wish absorbing the sun's warmth and leaving any tools you've brought to charge until you return home.

While power has a strong overtones from the Fire Element, the moon's symbolism can be used to encourage it as well, especially in metaphysical matters. In this case, you'll be doing a similar ritual to the first, only on each night of the full moon as it first appears in the sky.

Take your candle outside and light it as the moonlight reaches the Earth, saying:

"As the silvery beams, and the flame's glow,
As above, so below,
Power I wish for, power I'll know."

On the last night sit in the light of the moon and the candle, taking notes for your magickal grimoire or writing down any insights you receive about power and the wise use thereof.

When you need to "plug in" on the road (and it's not always possible to work in a private outdoor location) make this charm to carry with you. On any convenient Tuesday, light a red candle and focus on your goal. Take a AA or AAA battery (fully-charge), and wrap a strand of your hair around it. Drip some wax on the hair (to keep it in place), saying:

"By this Witch's hair and battery,
I hereby claim energy.
The spell held true by candlewick
And with my will the charm affix!"

Carry this with you when you know you'll be away from home for a while and may need a little extra energy. The charm works best if you hold it in your hand and recite the incantation to yourself. If the hair ever falls off, you need to remake the charm.

Protection

Plenty of people cast protection spells or enact safety rituals only *after* something has gone awry. I would recommend being a little more proactive than that. Our world is full of hazards. Heck, just getting out of bed can be tricky if you have children or pets who litter your floors with toys! Those who live in urban environments have the additional cumulative negativity of stressed-out people with which to cope. This is even more reason for protective Candle Magick that's enacted regularly as a spiritual vitamin to keep you safe and sound.

* ❄ Time your spells for when the moon is in Aries (cleansing) or Virgo (success), during hours of bright sunlight to banish the shadows, and the entire month of January (shielding energy).
* ❄ Add aromatics such as basil, cedar, hawthorn flowers, and woodruff flowers.

❈   Use a white candle (for Spirit and the white light of protection).

❈   Include other potential components and symbols associated with protection, such as eye agates, ash wood, bells, a Witch jar, cat's eye, drums, garlic, knots (to bind negativity), and the color red, which is considered abhorrent to ghosts and malicious fairies.

Candles make a lovely visual representation of the protective white light of which we often speak. For this activity, you'll need an object that represents the person or situation that needs protection. Then gather plenty of white candles so that they surround the symbolic item with an inward spiral of light energy (you want to direct the candle-power toward the object, not away from it).

Light these candles at dusk every night and leave them burning for a few minutes while you direct prayers or invocations on behalf of whatever you're directing energy toward. Continue until you know for certain that any potential harm has passed. Afterward, you might wish to melt the remaining candle wax again and make a shielding candle for that person (or to place in the situation) that can be lit if any issues arise again.

❧⁓❦⁓❧

Speaking of shielding candles, a simple way to protect your home is by designing special room candles. I suggest having four, each in the color of one of the Elements (yellow for East/Air, red for South/Fire, blue or purple for West/Water, and green or brown for North/Earth). For a few weeks before putting these around your house, wrap them in a soft cloth that's been dabbed with frankincense, pine, and sage oil. The wax will absorb the aroma, but it won't be overwhelming.

After they're scented, place the appropriate candle in its Elemental Quarter. Add an invocation so that when you light the candles, they create a semi-formal sacred space without fuss. Here's one example:

"Guardian of East and Air, protect this space
When your wick flares (light the East).
Guardian of the South and Fire, protect this space
When your flame grows higher (light the South).
Guardian of the West and Water, protect this space
Never let the light falter (light the West).
Guardians of the North and Earth, protect this space
when your sparks give birth (light the North).
Guardians in my sacred space, give shelter in all
storms...(standing in center).
No negativity is welcome here, and none may harm.
Stand watch in work, stand watch in play,
By night and noon, dark and day,
So be it."

Note: If you wish, you can have a fifth candle for Spirit (preferably white) somewhere centrally located to make all five points of the pentagram. Even when the candles are not lit, this type of energizing allows them to radiate an ambient protective energy.

Recovery (mental, physical, or spiritual)

The energy of recovery has dimensions: It aids someone when they're sick; It can bolster a sagging bottom line; It can provide support when one's spirit has been dragged through the proverbial mud of a difficult situation. Recovery spells are similar to healing spells except you're not only seeking reversal, but also forward progress (or minimally being back where you began instead of 10 paces behind that mark).

* Time your spells for waning moon (to decrease the power of the disease or problem), the

waxing moon to bring more positive energy to bear on the situation, and Thursdays (stamina) or Wednesdays (for ingenuity).

✳ Add aromatics such as lilac, apple, and nutmeg (or those more specifically geared to your needs—such as rose for an emotional recovery in a relationship).

✳ Use shoot green candles (the color of healthy, new growth).

✳ Include other potential components and symbols that you associate with recuperation and well being such as Band Aids, salve, soup, comfort foods, a red cross, etc.

Let's begin with a candle-powered potion as an overall tonic (physical realm). For this blend, you'll want some apple juice and a hint of nutmeg. Light a green candle near your working area to support the magick. Warm the apple juice on the stove stirring clockwise while saying:

"Where sickness dwells, heath impart,
Positive magick stays, all negativity depart.
Round the bowl, elixir true,
By my will, my health renew."

Pour this into a cup and move it to a spot where you can sit in the candle's renewing light. Sip slowly, letting the positive energy renew your body and spirit.

This activity's symbolism comes from the candleholder you'll be using. You'll need to find one of the thick squishy balls (the type that don't really hurt when they bounce off someone). Slice a little off the bottom so it will sit flat on a surface, and make a round hole in the top into which you can put a candle.

Next, carve your candle with the image of an eye or something else that you associate with mental functions. Dab this with a bit of rosemary oil and secure it in your holder. Light the candle saying:

> *"Within my mind, renewal start.*
> *Within my will, strength impart.*
> *No matter the distractions, no matter the attack,*
> *My mind and spirit like this flame—bounce back!"*

Keep this candle in a safe place and light it any time you feel as if your mental edge is waning. Note: If you choose, you can repeat the incantation five times when you light the candle—the number of awareness—to empower it further.

Having provided something for body and mind, let us also turn to your spirit and soul, which need as much tending as the other two portions of self. Earlier, we talked about making a house candle to honor the Spirit of a dwelling place. This activity is similar, but the Spirit for which you're creating the candle is your own.

Rather than using the traditional color and scent here, I suggest picking out your favorite colored wax and aromatics you find uplifting. In the bottom of whatever mold you'll be using, place a little coconut butter (this hardens similarly to wax and has salve-like qualities). Because you're focusing on recovery, make the candle during the full moon or at the noon hour for blessings.

As you melt the wax and add your aromatics, focus on wholeness of spirit. Add a simple chant that you can repeat all the while you're working such as:

> *"By my will and candle's flame,*
> *A renewal of spirit and soul I claim.*

When ere this candle burns,
Vitality to my spirit—returns!"

Let the candle set up, then keep it in a special spot for when you're feeling really lagging in spirit. Note: This candle also helps empower various forms of magick where you might feel your skills aren't quite "on."

Relationships

We've spoken of love, friendship, and passion—but what of other types of interactions? There are the relationships we have with coworkers, pets, family, and community. Some are good (some no so good) but, inevitably, times arise when we need to strengthen or heal our ties. Unfortunately, circumstances and distance don't always make that easy. Spells and rituals give you a media through which to answer the spiritual part of the equation while you continue your mundane efforts, no matter how far away a person or persons may be.

* Time your spells for the month of July or a Friday (if the relationship is of a romantic nature), when the moon is in Pisces (to inspire fruitful friendships), and a waxing to full moon (promotes good feelings between people).

* Add aromatics such as orange, rose, apple, basil, and lemon (all of which encourage warmth).

* Use a candle whose color implies the type of relationship for which you're working magick. A business relationship might require a brown or green color to represent the Earth Element and prosperity, for example.

* Include other potential components and symbols such as jade, knots, rings, cards, and forget-me-not type items.

Ever wish you could have just a glimmer of insight into a budding relationship? Candle scrying can help you predetermine a relationship's potential. For this activity, you need at least 15 minutes of quiet time, a candle whose color represents the potential partner, and a dark room. Please make sure there are no breezes here, as wind can wreak havoc on the results of a reading.

Begin by lighting the candle and getting comfortable somewhere nearby. If you can manage to have the candle's flame located around eye-height, that seems to work best. Think about the person you've recently gotten to know. Bring an image of him or her into your mind. Visualize the interactions you've had thus far, then focus on the question of what the most possible future holds for the two of you. (Note: I say "possible" future because your free will and actions from this moment forward can transform fate's web.)

Now, observe the flame's movements carefully. Try not to put your personal hopes and wishes into what you see. Simply observe.

Here is a brief list of interpretive values:

❋ **Sparking.** A potentially heated relationship either in terms of personalities that tend toward anger, or the spark of passion. If the sparks fly to the right, it's a more positive omen.

❋ **Smoldering.** Not much hope here. It will take plenty of effort to keep this relationship alive (especially if you want anything more than a short-term friendship or acquaintance).

❋ **Going out.** A truly negative sign. This relationship is going nowhere and may indeed be very bad for you. Note: If the candle burns for a few minutes before going out, it indicates you could have some fun times before the relationship ends.

* **Splitting in two at the top of the wick.** Twin flames with a solid body are a positive sign implying two people with one heart or goal.
* **Splitting completely.** An odd sign that says either someone intends to come between you or that obstacles lie in your path.
* **Dancing or burning very brightly.** A positive sign of good energy between you two.

To help heal a relationship, come together with a candle each and a breakable representation of the issues that stand between you. Light your personal candles to signal your peaceful intentions. Speak openly and honestly of whatever is bothering you (direct this not only to each other, but the object you've brought). Let that object absorb your negativity completely.

When you're both done speaking your minds, put the two breakable items together on a piece of paper or cloth (to catch the shards) and break them together. These should be buried or otherwise disposed of to put the negativity away. These matters are dead and buried.

Finally, blow out the candles and wrap them in a white cloth (to protect the new peace you've created). Tie the bundle together with three knots, representing you, your partner, and the relationship saying:

"Peace has been reclaimed.
By our promise—animosity released.
From this moment onward,
Love will never cease."

Keep the candles somewhere safe to use any time you need to bring some gentle salve to your relationship.

Separation

Separation spells are not solely for relationships. They're also intended to help you make transitions at the end of a job, before moving to a new residence, or breaking off a business partnership. The whole idea of a ritual or spell is one of closure, and to provide a positive new start.

❋ Time your spells for the Winter, dusk, and the dark moon.

❋ Add aromatics such as thyme for courage, myrrh for healing wounds, lotus to break the ties between you, sage for cleansing, and iris for wisdom.

❋ Use black candles (for endings) possibly coupled with green for a healthy separation or white for pure intentions.

❋ Include other potential components and symbols of separation such as a partition, a knife, or scissors. Also items that can be buried to mark a figurative death

For this activity you'll need to set up two candles with long strand of thread in front of them. One candle represents you and the other represents the person or situation from which you're separating. Mark each candle with an appropriate symbol before you begin.

Start with the candles setting close together (the string in front extends far beyond them on both sides). At dusk on night one, light them and separate the two about an inch, saying:

"Moving apart in body."

Blow out the candle (after focusing on the meaning of that phrase for a few minutes), turn, and walk away. Do not return to the candle until night two.

On the second night, light the two candles, and move them apart another inch saying:

"Moving apart in body, moving apart in mind."

Follow with your brief meditation, blow out the candle, and walk away. The third night follows the same pattern using the incantation:

"Moving apart in body, moving apart in mind, moving apart in spirit."

This time, before you blow out the candles, cut the string before them in half. Keep the half that was near your personal candle wrapped around that candle and store it away. The other half string and candle should be disposed of.

⁕⁕⁕

This activity is for a couple that wishes to use candle symbolism to help with their separation. In this case, you'll need three candles. Each person brings one candle, and the third represents the union. Each person should also bring symbols of the union that can be burned or destroyed in another fashion for a clean ending.

This activity begins as the first one did, at sundown with the central candle being lit. The couple should enter the room from opposite sides. Together, they light their individual candles from the union candle, saying:

"I accept my light back without anger or blame."

Next, the two should blow out the union candle together saying:

"We release our bonds mutually, with all good wishes."

At this point, if there's anything else positive the individuals wish to convey to each other, they should.

Finally, any symbols of the relationship can be ritually burned or put away (possibly by a third party). From this point, the couple turns away, walking out again in opposite directions not looking back. Symbolically, to look back holds on to the past. Learn from it, take the best, and leave the negativity firmly behind where it belongs.

Service (Charity)

"Life is no brief candle to me; it is a sort of splendid torch which I've got a hold of for the moment and I want to make it burn as brightly as possible before handing it on to future generations."

—George Bernard Shaw (1856–1950)

I know there have been many times when there was a need in our community that I wished I and others could meet more effectively. The elder or teacher who been on the road a long time needs service. The family whose main breadwinner has been unemployed for an extended time may need a little unobtrusive charity. In either case, both are important to keeping our Tribe whole. These spells are designed to encourage a generous heart and spirit wherever they're most needed.

* Time your spells as needed. Sunlight accents more mental/physical service while moonlight accents spiritual service.
* Add aromatics such as peach (for wisdom), marigold (for sensitivity/awareness), ginger (for energy), lavender (for harmony), and lily (for happiness).
* Use a candle whose color represents the individual or group toward whom you're directing the magick.
* Include other potential components and symbols such as a waitress styled tray, or

open hands (palm up). A good stone for spiritual service is sugilite, while tiger's eye helps the body, and fluorite assists the mind and skills.

This first spell is intended to open a community's heart to someone (or to a group) that has a specific need. Note: It is carefully contrived not to overstep free will, but rather illuminate the area of need.

Begin with a candle into which you've carved the name of the person or group in need. Place this on an altar or in another special spot and surround it with marigold petals, saying:

"Flowers of kindness surround you,
petals of gentle charity reach out to you,
budding consideration opens to you,
let every need be seen and met.
So mote it be."

Light this candle once a day at dawn (perhaps while you get ready for work), and repeat the incantation or meditate on the person or group toward whom this energy is directed. This is also a good time to do a little networking on their behalf (write emails, call, send a letter or two describing the need and how those you're contacting can help).

When the need passes, release the marigold petals to the four winds to bless the earth and others in need whose path they cross.

☙ ⸙ ❧

This activity allows you to direct spiritually supportive energy to a leader, elder, or teacher that needs a boost. You can use the other candle spell given here to accomplish this simply by changing the wording. However, I want to provide you with an alternative format with which to work.

If possible, have a picture of the person on hand (or something from them, such as a letter). Place a rainbow assortment of candles around this item (so that they can receive whatever type of energy they most need). Light these daily for a few minutes and say a brief prayer aimed toward that individual. Visualize them, and extend the energy of the flames and your words outward.

Save the remnant wax from those candles and remelt them during a full moon, adding some symbolic aromatics. Send this to the person if possible, or simply reuse the new candle to keep the positive energy going.

Sleep (rest)

Having three children and living in the city, I'm aware of the many things that can disrupt a person's sleep. I also live with an insomniac who goes through cycles of very uneven sleep patterns. This life experience brought about some personal ponderings about sleep and, in turn, the spells and charms that follow:

- ❋ Time your spells for right before bed for best results.
- ❋ Add calming aromatics such as chamomile, lavender, and mint.
- ❋ Use a purple candle (for a dreamy sleep), a white candle (for uninterrupted sleep), or blue candle (for overall calm).
- ❋ Include other potential components and symbols such as coral (specifically used for helping children sleep), or moonstone (better for adults). Also anything associated with sleep such as your pillow, favorite blanket, sheep (for counting), etc.

This activity begins with a warm lavender tea and by dressing your candle with lavender oil. Take about one-eighth of a cup of lavender and steep it in a cup of water (just the petals).

While that steeps, dress and light the candle. Breathe deeply. Lavender has a very relaxing quality. Hold the cup in both hands and empower the beverage by saying:

"Even as I drink this deep, bring to me a night of sleep."

Quaff the potion, blow out the candle, and let yourself float gently on the aroma of lavender off to sleep.

By the way, if you have some extra lavender flower, it's often beneficial to put a bundle of it (sachet size) under your pillow to keep the effect going all night.

❧ ⌥ ❧

For this activity, you'll need about eight light blue tapers and one other candle that represents the situation or person in need of tranquility. Each night around the time when most people are starting to relax, surround that central candle with the blue ones and light them while reciting calming words. For example, if you're working magick to help with your own sleeping patterns say:

"Stillness, calm, quite insure... bring to me a sleep that's pure."

To bring rest to a group that seems to be struggling, try:

"Goddess here my sincere behest,
Bring to_____some calm and rest!"

Leave the candles to burn for a while, and if possible remain there to direct the energy. Then, blow them out.

Continue this routine for as long as necessary to achieve results.

❧ ⌥ ❧

This sleep and dream charm is based on the Native American dream catchers. For it, you'll need a crocheted doily, a feather, a moonstone crystal bead, some thread, and, of course, a nice dark blue candle! During the waxing to full moon, decoratively attach the feather and crystal to the doily near the edge somewhere. As you sew these in place, repeat this incantation five times:

> *"On nights wings, sweet dreams my magick brings*
> *As moonstone shines, restful sleep will be mine!"*

Place the doily on a surface near to the bed. Put the dark blue candle atop this doily and light it every night before sleeping repeating the incantation. Take a few moments and meditate/relax before the candle, then blow it out and enjoy a peaceful night's sleep. By the way, because this activity tends to bring sweet dreams too, you may want to keep a tape recorder or pen and paper near the bed.

Travel

Travel spells focus on manifesting smooth, worry-free excursions. The next time you're taking a family outing, heading for a vacation, or have another adventure planned, enact these candlelit spells first so you have the most fun possible:

* Time your spells for just prior to your journey, or during the planning process.
* Add protective aromatics such as violet, clove, fennel, lilac, coconut, and sage.
* Use a white candle (for protection), or yellow (for movement).
* Include other potential components and symbols such as tin or turquoise (carried as amulets), maps and tour books, miniature vehicles, and corks with coins (for sea travel).

Make yourself a portable travel amulet. Begin with a white candle and a yellow candle into which you've carved the image of the type of vehicle you'll be using (you should make each one specifically). If you can also find a toy image to use for this charm all the better, but a suitable crystal will do along with some protective aromatics. Melt your candles in a non-aluminum pot over a low flame. Stir counterclockwise saying:

> *"From here to there, and there to here,*
> *Have no worries, have no fears,*
> *Home or away, away or home,*
> *In my_____I'll safely roam."*

Fill in the blank with the type of vehicle (car, bike, motorcycle, etc.).

When the wax is completely melted, add your aromatics. Let this cool until you can handle it easily. Shape the semi-warm wax around the crystal or toy token that represents the vehicle to surround it with protective energy. Place this into the vehicle. Note: If you live in a hot environment you may wish to wrap this bundle yet again with aluminum foil, waxed paper, or another protective wrap to keep it from melting and making a mess.

Save a few drops of wax from your first activity and mark your home on a map with it. Also mark the location to where you're traveling with the safety-charged wax. Now, take a toy car, plane, bus, or train and follow the route you'll be taking (if flying be as approximate as possible). Move the vehicle slowly and purposefully from home to the destination, saying:

> *"Adventure waits, I call on the Fates*
> *Protect my path, guide the way,*
> *Keep all dangers and delays at Bay!"*

Keep repeating this little chant all the while you move the vehicle. Then you can take both the map and the toy with you as amulets.

In Victorian times, people carried mint to encourage safe voyages. Blending this idea with Candle Magick isn't difficult. For this spell, begin with a grey candle that's been dressed with mint oil and a mint leaf. Light the candle visualizing the trip ahead (even if it's going to the office).

> *"Like the light of this candle surrounds,*
> *safety and protection abounds.*
> *Even when the flame ceases to shine,*
> *the magick within to this leaf binds.*
> (drip some wax on the mint leaf)
> *As the point between dark and day,*
> *this amulet to protect me*
> *Keep all dangers at bay."*

Tuck the mint leaf in your purse, wallet, or briefcase, then head out. By the way, it's not necessary to do this every morning. You can just light the candle while preparing for work and blow it out as you walk out the door. If the mint leaf becomes brittle and cracks, however, you should prepare a new one.

Transformation

> *"We must view young people not as empty bottles to be filled, but as candles to be lit."*
>
> —Robert H. Shaffer

Life is change. And these days, it seems as if changes come at warp speeds often leaving us breathless. We have to integrate plenty of external and internal transformations daily, and it certainly won't hurt to use a little candle-power to assist in that process. The purpose behind transformation spells include helping to process a change, getting some changes moving in the right direction, and adjusting to unwanted changes.

- ❄ Time your spells for midnight, dawn, and dusk (when time itself is transforming along with the light). New Year's Eve is also a good time.
- ❄ Add aromatics such as nutmeg (determination), orange (tenacity and luck), and balm (manifestation).
- ❄ Use any colored candle you prefer. The melting of the wax is, in itself, a strong symbol of change. However, you can choose the candle's color so it correlates to the area of your life where transformation is most needed.
- ❄ Include other potential components and symbols that have various states. For example, water can become steam or ice, tides shift and change, and crackers crumble. Eggs can be broken for breakfast or hatched. Caterpillars become butterflies. Also consider tools that help us transform things from one state to another (the blender or food processor makes things liquid).

For this activity, begin with a piece of soft clay and a carefully preserved eggshell filled with dirt, a flowering seed, and a birthday candle on top (the birthday candle is held in place by the dirt). Make a thumbprint impression in the clay that will hold the eggshell upward for the duration of the spell.

Wait until dawn (for a positive change) and light the candle, saying:

"As dawn gives way to day... light the way, light the way. As my path is rearranged—help me accept gentle change."

Blow out the candle as you would for any wish and set it aside. Take the eggshell out to some good soil where you can tend it and plant it in the ground. By the time the seed begins to sprout your transitions should be rolling along smoothly.

❧ ⸙ ❧

I have frequently found Butterfly-shaped candles at dollar stores and gift shops. These are ideal for transformation magick. Even if you can't find one, you can carve the image of a butterfly onto a candle of your choice. Use this as the starting point for a candlelight visualization.

As you look into the flame, imagine that glow getting larger and larger—surrounding you like a cocoon. It's warm and comforting. You know you're wholly safe. Within this energy shell, you can make whatever shifts in awareness or thinking that you most need. Take your time. Breathe deeply. Don't rush this process.

As you're working through those items, imagine yourself growing wings even as the butterfly you carved on the candle. The light around you gathers and shapes them— these are wings of power and light...and life! By the end of the visualization, the energy that surrounded you at first has wholly poured itself into your spiritual wings so that you can lift yourself above circumstances and find success.

❧ ⸙ ❧

This activity takes place at a beach at sunset. The visual effect is really beautiful, but if you can't get to a beach you can use a box of sand, a candle, and any water source instead. Wait for the sun to glow warmly on the horizon's edge. Light your candle, using the beach to hold it erect. Speak your needs and wishes into the water.

Next, find a spot nearby to sit, watch, and wait. Let yourself be filled by the ever-moving waters that shift with ease. Become as the flow that fills any shape. If possible, stay until the water extinguishes the candle, and gather up a little sand and wax to keep in a pouch as a charm that keeps the magick moving with you.

Truth

Truth can be a very subjective thing, but there are times when you need harsh objectivity and a reality check. When you sense you may not be getting the whole picture, or something is "too good to be true," shine a light on it with these candle-crafted spells and divinations:

* Time your spells for when the stars are shining, or when the moon is full.
* Add aromatics such as peach (insight), saffron (wisdom), rose (foresight), and mint (clarity and awareness).
* Use a white candle.
* Include other potential components and symbols, such as bloodstone and malachite (discernment), the earth (people used to vow honesty with one hand on the ground), binoculars (or anything that magnifies), a mirror (for self-truth), and owls (the messengers of truth).

Enact this spell five hours before you go on a fact-finding mission. Begin with five white candles. Come the first hour, light the first candle, saying:

> *"One: the light of truth to saver,*
> *and from it I shall not waiver."*

Come the second hour, light the second candle from the first, saying:

> *"One: the light of truth to saver,*
> *and from it I shall not waiver*
> *Two: the glow of honest words,*

Spirit listen—let my prayer be heard."

Come the third hour, light the third candle from the first and second, saying

"One: the light of truth to saver,
and from it I shall not waiver.
Two: the glow of honest words,
Spirit listen—let my prayer be heard.
Three: the flame of sincerity,
through all lies let my eyes see."

The fourth and fifth hour follow the same pattern with these additional verses:

"Fourth: the glimmer of something hidden or sealed,
by this magick, let all be revealed.
Fifth: the spark of good intent
from will to world my spell is sent."

If you wish, you can take some wax drippings with you from all five candles as a truth talisman.

☽ ༺ ☾

Go to a dusty surface with a candle and a soft cloth. Set the candle down, light it, then rub the surface counter clockwise saying

"Uncertainty erase, the truth to face,
Reality shine, by this spell the truth will be mine."

Note: You're not really trying to clean the surface here, but rather to create a swirling pattern in the dust. Now stop and scry the surface using the candle's reflection on the surface. Think of the situation in which you feel you're not getting the whole truth. Watch for images to appear in the swirls or specific movements. Movement upward and to the right of the image means *yes,* you're not getting all the information you need. Movement downward or left means *no,* everything is as it seems. Clockwise inward moving spirals mean you're getting closer to the truth, while outward counterclockwise ones mean that you're looking in the wrong direction.

Unconscious Mind

Jung talked about the collective unconscious among humans—the well of information and knowledge to which we all have access. This theory explains why various people all get the same idea even when separated by miles, cultural differences, and even time. We cannot begin to tap this well when we can't even begin to know our own subconscious and super-consciousness. In spiritual traditions, it's important to remain aware that there is a lot going on, that the conscious mind doesn't always register. In effect, we file it into the subconscious to be retrieved in dreams, visions, and those periodic light-bulb moments when we say, "ah ha!" These spells are designed to help the user get back in touch with the inner worlds where mind and spirit interact more readily.

* Time your spells for when the moon is waxing to full, or Monday (the moon's day).
* Add lunar and psychic aromatics such as bay, honeysuckle, lemongrass, marigold, mint, rose, vanilla, and thyme.
* Use silver or white candles to represent the moon.
* Include other potential components and symbols of the higher self and spiritual pursuits such as silver, moonstone, cat's eye, rowan, or willow wood.

Awakening your latent skills and insights takes practice. Thankfully, candles are inexpensive tools with which to practice. Specifically, you can learn to hone your intuitive self by making wax patterns on paper or water.

Begin by drawing an eye on piece of paper. Place this paper on a tabletop and think of a simple question. Next take a yellow candle that is lit and hold it over the paper saying:

"Knowledge be clear by candlelight
Grant to me the gift of site!"

Put the candle aside and look at the paper, especially around the eye. Let your vision blur slightly and then make notes of any impressions you get. The patterns or pictures can be looked up in any dream dictionary or other divinatory correspondence list. The idea here is to hone your ability to tap the unconscious mind by using it more often.

If you decide you'd like to try the water approach instead, place a clear bowl of water on top of the drawing of the eye or perhaps a window (to open inner windows of Self). Then, simply drip the wax (more than one color if you wish) into the water and look for the emerging patterns. This time, try an incantation while you're looking at the surface, like:

"From my spirit nothing is sealed,
In this wax insights revealed!"

☙ ⸙ ❧

Another good way to empower the unconscious and intuitive self is through this meditation. Go outside on a night when you can see the moon clearly. Take your candle with you (anointed with an aromatic of your choice). Get comfortable and look at the candle as you begin to breathe deeply and relax. Make sure you can visualize the candle's flame clearly in your mind before you close your eyes.

Now, the main chakras governing the unconscious/ superconscious mind are those of the heart, third eye, and crown. Your heart center is located in the middle of your chest; the third eye, between your eyes on your forehead;

and the crown is where a baby's soft spot would be in an adult. Begin at the heart center, visualizing the flame of your candle setting right in front of it. Let the light be wholly absorbed by that region (you'll feel warm or tingly).

Next, move the flame in front of the third eye chakra. See the warm flames swirling clockwise inward overflowing it with energy. Finally, move the flame to your crown chakra, and let the energy sprinkle down over you like rain. Continue as long as you wish, and make notes of your experience afterward.

Victory (success)

The ego is an important element to human awareness. While none of us wants it running amok, having self-confidence and a sense of true success in specific areas of our life is healthy and necessary. Nonetheless, there are times when our daily reality hands us proverbial lemons. When you want your resulting lemonade to be all the sweeter, and that victory to finally arrive after all your hard work, bring some magick into the equation for just the right push.

- Time your spells for dawn or Spring (when light overcomes darkness). Also the blue moon is a good time (especially if you need a figurative miracle).
- Add successful aromatics such as lemon, cinnamon, ginger, and pine.
- Use gold or silver candles (gold for larger successes). Alternatively, vibrant yellow or orange will work.
- Include other potential components and symbols that represent victory. For example, blue ribbons imply winning a competition. Other fortunate components include agates, hematite, amber, bloodstone, and any items bearing solar imagery.

This spell is delightfully simple. Right before you know you're going into a situation where you need a real victory, take out a candle and dab it with a bit of lemon essence. If possible, place this candle where it can safely burn unattended while you're going about the necessary task(s). Light the candle, saying:

"As the candle burns brighter,
Bring the success desired."

Repeat the incantation eight times to build strong foundations, then move forward with confidence.

❧ ❦ ❧

For this activity, we're going to begin by using the symbolic value of a blue ribbon braided with that of gold (solar/blessings), and a gold candle. Light the gold candle so it shines while you're working. Take two blue ribbons to one central gold and as you braid them, recite this little verse repeatedly until you're done:

"Ribbons of blue, the victory's mine.
Ribbon of gold, my skills how they shine.
Magick within, braided and bound,
A victory, sure, will soon come round!"

Drop a bit of wax on the ribbon's ends so they don't fray, and carry this token as a success charm. Note: You can now light the candle and repeat the incantation to further support the charm, or possibly use it to burn paper images of anything that you feel is holding you back from a clean victory.

Virtue (honor)

The importance of the words honor, respect, and gratitude has already been stressed. Honor and virtue are not outmoded values for the true spiritual seeker. When one honors something, they are much less likely to abuse it (and, in fact, will appreciate it all the more). Virtue is our guiding light in how to act and react every moment of every day. Now, as lofty as that sounds, there are days when I want to toss all my ideals out the window because of a perceived injustice or harm. While there may be times to take up arms and fight, these spells are intended for those moments when you need to reconnect with your own sense of right and wrong, and stand by it without fail.

* Time your spells for daylight hours (honor never hides in the shadows).

* Add aromatics such as thyme (courage), nutmeg (holding firm to a belief), cedar (protection), and marigold (justice).

* Use a white candle for pure motivation and thoughtful action.

* Include other potential components and symbols that represent these qualities to you (I use the image of a knight or his lady's favor, as one example). Also, any white pieces of clothing can imply virtue (purity).

When you're not sure what the best, most honorable decision is, this is a nice, candlelit prayer that you can say every morning and evening until the choice becomes clear. Start by lighting the candle of your choice, then say:

"Light of spirit, light of truth
illuminate the way between right and wrong
Let my path be sure, my will be strong
Show me where my efforts belong
Spirit of truth, Spirit of light
Help me make the choice that's right!"

Pay particular attention to any dreams you have during the period you're enacting this spell, as they may reveal your best course of action.

This is a little chant that can go with you anywhere. When you face a situation where there's the temptation to do something you know is wrong, bring to your mind's eye the image of a white candle to provide energy and to light your way in the murky waters that surround. Then silently or out loud say:

> *"The effect of respect*
> *Is an attitude of gratitude!*
> *Honor, goodness, and trust*
> *In my actions are MUST!"*

Continue to repeat this to yourself until you find that knee jerk reaction calming so you can walk away having your karma intact.

Weather

As the old saying goes, if you want the weather to change, wait five minutes. Or, you could cast a spell! I share weather-oriented spells with a warning. Bear in mind that you're playing with the patterns of an entire world. By trying to play push-me, pull-you with a storm front, you could be robbing an area of much needed water (as an example). So think carefully about what you need, when you need it, and why. To provide a personal illustration, I was performing an outdoor wedding for a dear friend and a serious storm was prevailing. Rather than try to stop it, I asked for a one-hour holding pattern in my magick. It worked perfectly (but I got only 60 minutes—not one second more!). This met the need without completely disrupting Mother Nature.

Because different types of weather require different candle colors and aromatics, refer to the following section (set up according to) the weather desired:

✳ **Rain.** When you want to bring rain, sprinkle damp heather around a lighted candle (so it appears to be raining), then blow it out (water douses fire). Add an incantation to this process that indicates the amount of rain desired, and for how long for best results. If you want to make a portable rain charm, use the same candle, gather up a bit of heather, and put it in a pouch with a quartz crystal and a few drops of wax. Release all but the candle to a living water source to invoke rain.

✳ **Sun.** To clear away the clouds in a sky, begin by lighting a yellow or gold candle to honor the sun. Then take a piece of kelp or any Water-oriented stone and bury it in sand or dirt (this also quells wind). To that foundation you can certainly add a chant, for example, the childhood rhyme of "rain, rain, go away," which works as a perfectly viable invocation.

✳ **Snow or mist.** Living in Western New York, it's hard to imagine anyone wanting snow, but should this be a desire, light a white candle then take it along with a piece of jade and toss the stone in living water. You can stay in that location with the candle held high (lighting the way for weather spirits) and add an invocation should you wish.

✳ **Wind.** To raise a wind, light a yellow candle (this honors the Air Element). Then toss either some saffron or broom toward the East with a simple invocation such as:

"Let the winds begin!"

Alternatively, you can make a wind rope like the Arabs used to by binding a piece of broom or saffron with a drop of yellow wax into the rope. Make three knots this way. Unleash one knot when you want a light breeze, two for a fuller forced wind. Do not release the third—that is considered greedy.

Wisdom

"To light one candle to God and another to the Devil is the principle of wisdom."

—Jose Bergamin

Ah, my kingdom to have been wiser much younger. There are so many situations that challenge our sagacity: Making decisions in child rearing, choosing a Path, dealing with co-workers, balancing the budget. Any of these moments provides an opportunity to put the symbolism of candles to work yet again.

* Time your spells according to the area of life in which you need wisdom. For example, wisdom on your spiritual Path is best accomplished by working with a full moon, whereas conscious wisdom for daily tasks is more solar in Nature.
* Add aromatics such as iris, peach, and sage, all of which support this goal.
* Use purple candles (especially for spiritual wisdom).
* Include other sagacious potential components and symbols such as an owl. Among stones we find jade (especially for wisdom in relationships), sodalite, and sugilite. Edible items include almonds, peaches, and olives.

Use this potion for balanced wisdom. Begin with a dark purple candle lit in the kitchen while you're working. When you ignite the candle, say:

"Wisdom's light shine, within and without,
Conscious wisdom be mine!"

Next, take some peach juice (you can find this type of blend in most frozen food sections or natural food cooperatives). Leave this adjacent to the candle in a sunny window of the kitchen for about five minutes to absorb the light. Blow out the candle, and put the glass of juice away until evening.

When the moon rises, repeat the procedure, but altering the incantation to:

"Wisdom's light shine, within and without,
Intuitive wisdom be mine!"

Again, leave these two items in the moonlight for a few minutes, then drink the juice to internalize the energy. By the way, if you can't find juice, a fresh peach works effectively, too.

❧ ☙ ✦ ☙ ❧

To bring wisdom into your profession, find two nice candleholders, a purple candle, and one candle that represents your work. Carve the purple candle with an image of an eye (for example, the eye of Ra) for insight. Carve the other candle with an image of your profession (if you're a writer, carve a quill or pen, for example).

On the three nights of the full moon, enact this spell. Place the two candles across from each other on a table or altar. Each night as the moon rises, light the business candle from the wisdom candle, saying:

"Like this candle's light
My wisdom shines bright!"

Afterward, move the candles slightly closer together and let them burn for fourty minutes (four being an Earth-oriented number). On the second and third nights repeat as the first, but by the third night the candles should be sitting side by side. When the 40 minutes are completed, blow out the candles and bind them together. If possible keep these at your place of work or store them with symbols of your problem.

Wishes

Children and adults from all walks of life practice wishing. It is one of the most user-friendly forms of will-driven magick. And considering at least one of those forms of wishing comes in blowing out birthday candles, why not take the whole concept further? If the lighting of a candle indicates our intention, then its flame and smoke can send our wishes out to the Universe.

    ❋   Time your spells for when the stars are shining, or when the moon is full.

    ❋   Add aromatics typically associated with wishing such as sage, sandalwood, and violet.

    ❋   Use a candle whose color represents the area of your life to which the wish is directed.

    ❋   Include other potential components and symbols on which people wish such as coins, birthday candles, and four leaf clovers.

This wish spell is simple and only requires that you have a bay leaf and a candle of a suitable color to your goal. Write a word on the bay leaf that describes your wish. Light this in the flame of your candle saying:

"By the candlelight, wish take to flight
Burned by the Fire, my wishes go higher
In the smoke it's free, so mote it be!"

Note: You will want to have a small fireproof container nearby that you can put the bay leaf in to burn up completely. Continue chanting while it burns, then release the ashes to the four winds, trusting the energy to manifest.

This is a fun adaptation of the French tradition of floating candles with wishes. You can enact it on a pool or in the stream of a hose, but a river, lake, or ocean seem to work better (for example, living water sources). For this, you'll need a child's toy boat (preferably a wooden one so that it's biodegradable). Alternatively, you can make a float for your candle by binding popsicle sticks together, raft style, or use a floating candle.

On top of this foundation, put a small votive candle dabbed with an oil corresponding to your goal. Light the candle, then gently launch the ship on the chosen water, saying:

> *"By will and wish, by wish and will,*
> *The light of this candle shall fulfill*
> *As it floats out of sight*
> *I extend my wish, with all my might*
> *The light of hope on currents strong*
> *Take my wish where it belongs."*

Continue reciting the rhyme until you can no longer see the candle.

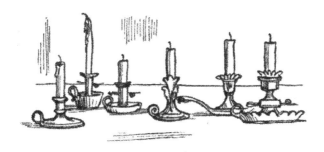

Afterword

This exploration of Candle Magick has been fun and challenging for me. There were times while I was writing when I thought, *"What else can I possibly do with a candle?"* As you can see, candles certainly withstood that creative dare with a unique flare, and truly surprised me. They are an incredibly flexible tool that no Witch's kit is complete without.

I hope you find these ideas helpful, that they inspire more of your own, and that, akin to the candle in the dark, you shine this knowledge and magick into the world. With that thought, I leave you these wonderful words:

> *"Sound when stretched is music.*
> *Movement when stretched is dance.*
> *Mind when stretched is meditation.*
> *Life when stretched is celebration."*

—Shri Shri Ravishankar Jee

Appendix A:
Historical Tidbits,
Folk Beliefs,
& Helpful Hints

Historical Tidbits and Fact-Findings

※ History indicates that Egyptians were the first people to make and use candles around the fourth century B.C.E.

※ Candles are mentioned in Biblical writings as early as the 10th century B.C.

※ By canon law, candles used in certain rituals of the Roman Catholic Church must contain not less than 51 percent beeswax. The remainder may be a vegetable or a mineral wax, but not tallow.

※ Greek and Romans were the first to add wicks to the candle's construction.

※ Candles have been made out of a multitude of base materials including tallow, insect wax, seed wax, bayberry, whale Spermaceti, palm leaves, candlefish, paraffin, and cerio tree wax.

※ The simplest (and smelliest) candles known as rush light were made by dipping rushes in leftover kitchen fat.

❋ The first dipped candles, made with beeswax, originated in the 1200s, followed by molded candles in the 1400s, and then by automated candle-making machines in the 1800s.

❋ The English Tallow Chandlers were incorporated in 1462 and they regulated trade in candles made from animal fats.

❋ Some of the more advanced candle-makers would bleach their candles by hanging them outside for as long as eight to 10 days.

❋ Pioneer homes achieved fancy striped effects by using the red juice of pokeberries, green from wild nettles, yellow from alder bark, and other natural dyestuffs.

❋ In 1834, inventor Joseph Morgan introduced a machine, that allowed continuous production of molded candles by the use of a cylinder, which featured a movable piston that ejected candles as they solidified.

❋ Also in the 19th century, changes took place in the design of the wicks used in candles. Instead of being made by simply twisting strands of cotton, wicks were now plaited tightly. As a result, the burned portion curled over and was consumed, rather than falling messily into the melting wax.

❋ The term *candlepower* is based on a measurement of the light produced by a pure spermaceti candle weighing one-sixth of a pound, burning at a rate of 120 grams-per-hour.

❋ America's first contribution to candle-making was when they discovered that boiling the grayish green berries of bayberry bushes produced a sweet-smelling wax that burned cleanly.

❄ The first "standard candles" were made from spermaceti wax. Spermaceti was obtained through a crystallization process, and it did not elicit a repugnant odor when burned. Furthermore, spermaceti wax was found harder than both tallow and beeswax.

❄ Currentlly there are well over 3,000 types of candles available to businesses and individuals, produced by some 300 manufacturers.

❄ U.S. candle consumer retail sales for 2001 are projected at $2.3 billion, not including candle accessories.

❄ Candles can range in retail price from approximately 50¢ for a votive candle to around $75 for a large column candle although a specialty candle could be as much as $200.

❄ Candle manufacturers' surveys show that 96 percent of all candles purchased are bought by women.

❄ Candles are used in seven out of 10 U.S. households. A majority of consumers burn candles for less than three hours per occasion. A majority of consumers also burn candles between one to three times per week, with half of these consumers burning one to two candles at a time.

Folk Beliefs

❄ The gift of a candle to newlyweds insures them of providence and fertility.

❄ Lighting a candle with your right hand brings luck.

❄ Letting candles burn out naturally, especially on special occasions, improves good fortune.

※ To avoid problems, never light more than two candles from one match.

※ Bayberry candles presented on New Year's bring health and money.

※ A candle that goes out without explanation is either a bad omen, or indicates the presence of a restless ghost.

※ A candle that refuses to light portends a storm on the horizon (note the storm can be figurative, like emotional).

※ Candle flames that shape themselves into the form of a ring predict a forthcoming marriage, in the household.

※ A burning candle placed inside a hollowed out pumpkin or jack-o'-lantern on Samhain works to keep evil spirits and demons at bay.

※ For good luck, burn black and orange candles on Halloween, then gaze into them to see the future.

※ If a candle falls and breaks in two, double trouble will come to you.

※ To dream of a white candle portends true love.

※ Seeing two candles in a dream is a sign of a forthcoming a marriage proposal.

※ A red candle in a dream symbolizes passion and sexual desire.

※ To dream of five candles predicts love and marriage.

※ To dream of a candle set firmly in a holder is an omen of happy and prosperous future.

※ To dream of a candleholder without a candle in it foretells sorrow.

- Always light candles at moments of birth, marriage and death. This keeps malevolent spirits away.
- Light a brown candle Candlemas for protection against ghosts.
- In Sicily, fishermen burn ornate candles for their patron saint to obtain blessings.
- A pink candle burned on Valentine's Day inspires love and devotion.
- A burning candle placed in a window will ensure the safe return of a lover traveling abroad.
- To test the fidelity of a lover, light a candle outdoors near his or her house. If the flame burns towards you the lover is faithful.
- To reclaim the affections of a lost lover, thrust two pins or needles through the wick of a burning candle as you say his or her name.
- Light a green candle on a night of the new moon for prosperity.
- To light a candle from the hearth fire prevents wealth.

Helpful Hints

- Remove candle wax from fabric by laying newspaper over it and placing a warm iron (set on low) over top and rubbing gently. Repeat, allowing the paper to absorb the melted wax.
- To dispose of unwanted wax, pour the liquid into a milk carton for garbage disposal.
- Soft cloths can remove minor bits of dirt or scratches from stored candles.

* Chilling candles or washing them in cold water first helps them to burn evenly and last longer (freezing also retains the aroma).

* If a candle looses its aroma, just dab it with some essential oil.

* Wrap scented candles and store them separately from others to keep the aromas from mixing.

* Trim candle wicks to one-fourth of an inch to avoid soot marks on the ceiling of a room.

* Use a piece of aluminum foil in the bottom of a candle holder to help keep a wobbly candle steady.

* When the sides of a pillar candle get too high and extinguish the wick, simply trim back the top of the candle and save the remnants for making another taper!

* When you are short on time and still want to do a candle spell, use a birthday candle!

* The budget-minded Witch can go to dollar stores to get inexpensive candles, holders, and even aromatic oils.

* If possible, get yourself the "aim and flame" type of lighter for Candle Magick. This will keep you from burning your fingers, especially on hard to reach wicks.

Appendix B:
Useful Correspondences

Colors

If you wish to use natural colorings when making home-made candles, the magickal correspondence of the plants used then add to the energy. Rose coloring comes from bloodroot (protection, love), a gold color can be obtained from the oxeye daisy (Fire/solar energy), tansy leaves (health) yield a green hue, myrrh (spirituality, Well-being) provides orange tinting and marigold (dreams,psychicism) makes yellow.

Candle Color	Astrological Signs	Attributes, Weekdays, and Stones
Black	Virgo, Libra, Capricorn	Banishing, quiet, restfulness, grief, acceptance, parting. Use on Saturday with jet or obsidian.
Blue	Aquarius, Gemini, Libra, Pisces, Virgo	Peace, comprehension, patience, noble ideals, opportunity, trust, truth, justice. Use on Thursday with lapis or turquoise.

Brown	Capricorn, Scorpio, Cancer	Grounding, Earth energies, fate, resolution, hearth and home, balance, foundations, acceptance, Use on Saturday with brown agate or tiger's eye.
Gold	Leo, Virgo, Sagittarius	Solar Magick, god-oriented, victory, overcoming, improved outlooks, wealth, honor, longevity, ambition. Use on Sunday with yellow-colored crystals.
Grey	(any)	Neutrality, invisibility, compromise. Use any day with gray banded agate.
Green	Aquarius, Pisces, Cancer, Virgo	Growth, health, money, luck, sympathy, Earth Magick, tonic qualities. Use on Fridays with jade moss agate.
Orange	Sagittarius	The harvest, encouragement, joy, motivation, fertility, self-confidence, abundance. Use on Sunday with crystals, such as carnelian.
Pink	Taurus, Aries	Friendship, honor, goodness, peace, romance, emotional healing, sleep, forgiveness. Use on Friday with rose quartz.
Purple	Aquarius, Pisces, Libra	Spirituality, wisdom, psychism, dream work, happiness, comprehension, spiritual healing. Use on thursday with amethyst or sugilite.
Red	Taurus, Gemini, Leo, Aries, Scorpio	power, passion, health, courage, Fire Element, energy, tenacity, mental keenness, strength, overcoming. Use on Tuedsay with red crystals such as jasper.

Silver	Cancer	Moon Magick, goddess-oriented, divination, astral work, insight. Use on Monday with white-colored stones.
White	Pisces, Aries	Cleansing, truth, purity, enthusiasm, healing, goddess energy, focus, protection, consecration, connecting with spirit guides, beginnings. Use on Monday in combinatiton with clear quartz or white stones.
Yellow	Taurus, Leo, Sagittarius, Gemini	Communications, certainty, Air Element, business improvements, improved memory and consentration, the conscious mind. Use on Wednesday with citrine.

** NOTE: Various sources disagree on the astrological associations for colors. I have printed the most common ones found, but please trust your instincts.

Numbers

Numbers can be carved into candles. Alternatively, an incantation can be repeated a supportive number of times, or a candle and components left to charge for a symbolic number of hours or minutes.

1: Personal Magick, completion, the number representing solar energy.

2: United effort, cooperation, partnership.

3: The body-mind-spirit trinity, fortitude.

4: Earth, cycles, foundations, money matters.

5: Alertness, awakenings, the Elements in balance.

6: Tenacity, completion, protection.

7: Water, the moon, diversity, perspective.

8: Leadership, changes, logical mind, concrete reality.

9: Giving to receive, service, the mysteries.

10: Solar and god energies.

Stones

Use stones in, on, or near your candles to both support the magick, and so that you have a portable talisman after the working to keep the energies close at hand.

Agate: protection, Gardening Magick, Earth-oriented energies.

Amber: health and "storing" energy.

Amethyst: self-control, truth, psychism.

Bloodstone: stress-relief, restoring emotional balance.

Carnelian: overall tonic qualities, blessings, hope, honesty.

Coral: Water energies, protection of children, improved perspectives.

Fluorite: effective application of one's skills, confidence.

Jade: love, protecting relationships.

Jasper: weather working.

Lapis: spirituality and meditation.

Malachite: precognition.

Moonstone: lunar energy, nurturing, awareness, luck.

Quartz: good all-purpose stone (clear quartz).

Rose Quarts: self-love, gentle feelings, friendship.

Tourmaline: creativity, banishing fear, inner-peace.

Turquoise: safe travel, communication.

Shapes and Images

For carving into the candles or making into part of an amulet, charm or talisman (preferably in a wax base):

Almond shape: Spiritual energy (feminine).

Anchor: sability.

Ankh: health and longevity.

Arrow: guiding energy, accomplishment.

Circle: the moon or sun, cycles, safety.

Crescent moon: protection from evil.

Cross (or X): Elemental Balance, reaching goals successfully.

Dollar sign: Prosperity Magick.

Eye: understanding, vision, comprehension.

Feather: Air Element.

Hexagram: the connection between the spiritual and temporal.

Hourglass: time's movement.

Key: opening, opportunity, unlocking a mystery.

Knot: binding or loosing energy.

Line: singularity; the Path.

Runes: This depends on the rune (each of which has it's own value), but all are easily carved.

Shield: bravery, safety, agility.

Smile: happiness.

Spiral: growing or decreasing energies (outward moving spiral grows, inward declines).

Square: Earth energy (see the number four).

Star: Wish Magick, universal patterns, fulfillment.

Triangle (upward): Fire Element, body-mind-spirit balance.

Web: networking.

Aromatics and Herbs

Aromatics and herbs can be brewed into your home made candles, rubbed into prefabricated ones, become part of portable charms, or blended into potions for external application (or consumption, **if edible**).

Allspice: prosperity, health, warm feelings.

Angelica: protection.

Almond: joy, self-control.

Apple: harmony, health, insightfulness.

Basil: love, peace, and safety.

Bayberry: good fortune and abundance.

Berry (any): abundance.

Borage: bravery and improved perspectives.

Cedar: money and cleansing.

Chamomile: calmness, easing stress, improved sleep.

Cinnamon: abundance, relationships.

Clove: love.

Clover: luck and financial improvements.

Dill: protection (especially for children), rest.

Fennel: banishing people or situations that bug you.

Frankincense: bravery, luck, wealth (also good for purification).

Ginger: energy, health, victory.

Heather: good fortune, dedication, Weather Magick, fertility.

Honeysuckle: intuitiveness, abundance, protection.

Jasmine: passion, inventiveness.

Lavender: peace, anti-stress, harmony.

Lemon: devotion, longevity.

Marjoram: joy.

Mint: safety in travel, money, health.

Myrrh: wisdom, spiritual focus, meditative aid.

Nutmeg: psychic awareness.

Orange: faithfulness, love.

Peach: sagacity, joy.

Pine: wellness, cleansing.

Rose: devotion, love, trust.

Rosemary: dedication, memory, love.

Sage: wisdom and longevity.

Sandalwood: symmetry, strength, calmness, psychic awareness.

Thyme: bravery and communing with fairies.

Vanilla: energy boost, improved awareness.

Timing

The ancients often used propitious timing to aid their efforts. For our purposes, the days of the week and phases of the moon are the easiest things to follow for symbolic value and ease of application.

Weekdays:

❃ Monday: white or silver (or very pale blue on a blue moon).

The best day of the week to work Candle Magick for dreaming, working through emotions, gardens, health, cleansing, fertility, goddess oriented efforts, and psychism.

* Tuesday: red or pink.
The best day of the week to work Candle Magick for turning away negative energy purposefully aimed at you, determination, legal matters, expansion, bravery, improved physical strength, and finances.

* Wednesday: purple.
The best day of the week to work Candle Magick for improved success in business, courage, clarity, safety abroad, the muse, and opening the lines of communication.

* Thursday: dark blue.
The best day of the week to work Candle Magick for love, promise making, loyalty, divination, justice, noble ideals, commitment, and respect.

* Friday: green or yellow.
The best day of the week to work Candle Magick for developing or improving long-term relationships, kinship, personal growth, peace, passion, and social pleasure.

* Saturday: brown or black.
The best day of the week to work Candle Magick for growth, liberation, safety, tying up loose ends, banishing sadness, psychic self-defense, and the longevity of any project.

* Sunday: yellow, gold, orange.
The best day of the week to work Candle Magick for god-oriented efforts, glamoury,

inventiveness, individuality, self-awareness, logic, hope, success, luck, and learning.

Moon Phases:

❄ Blue moon: overcoming great obstacles; the seemingly miraculous.

❄ Dark moon: weeding out unproductive habits, releasing the past, rest, secrecy.

❄ Full moon: manifestation, completion, water-oriented energy.

❄ New moon: beginnings, slow but steady increase.

❄ Waning moon: decrease, banishing, closure, lessening, endings.

❄ Waxing moon: growth-oriented energy, increase, success, fertility.

Sun Phases:

❄ Dawn: inception, hope, change, increase, joy.

❄ Noon: blessings, energy, success, the god aspect.

❄ Dusk: completion, closure, endings, release.

❄ Midnight: the Witching hour, balance, the goddess aspect.

Seasons:

❄ Spring: flowering of new skills, hopefulness, friendship, gentle love, trust, overcoming negativity, change, a fresh start.

❊ Summer: fertility, power, strength, healing,
   illumination, banishing darkness, personal
   empowerment and fulfillment.

❊ Fall: justice, harvesting what you've sown,
   the on-going abundance of Earth, cleansing,
   conservation (frugality), balance.

❊ Winter: the home, family, health,
   purification, rest, renewal, completion or
   closure, overcoming fear, goodwill, charity.

Bibliography

Aldington, Richard translator. *New Larousse Encyclope dia of Mythology.* Middlesex, England: Hamlyn Publishing, 1973.

Ann, Martha & Imel, Dorothy Myers. *Goddesses in World Mythology.* New York, NY: Oxford University Press, 1995.

Beyerl, Paul. *Herbal Magick.* Custer, WA: Phoenix Publishing, 1998.

Bruce-Mitford, Miranda. *Illustrated Book of Signs & Symbols.* New York, NY: DK Publishing, 1996.

Buckland, Raymond. *Advanced Candle Magick.* St. Paul, MN: Llewellyn Publications, 1996.

———. *Practical Candleburning Rituals.* St. Paul, MN: Llewellyn Publications, 1970

Budge, E. A. Wallis. *Amulets & Superstitions.* Oxford, England: Oxford University Press, 1930.

Cavendish, Richard. *A History of Magic.* New York, NY: Taplinger Publishing, 1979.

Cristiani, R. S. *Perfumery & Kindred Arts.* Baird and Company, PA: 1877.

Culpeper's Herbal, D. Potterton, editor. Sterling
     Publishing, NY 1983

Cunningham, Scott. *Crystal, Gem & Metal Magic*. St.
     Paul, MN: Llewellyn Publications, 1995.

————. *Encyclopedia of Magical Herbs*. St. Paul, MN:
     Llewellyn Publications, 1988.

————. *Magic in Food*. St. Paul, MN: Llewellyn
     Publications, 1991.

Davison, Michael Worth, editor. *Everyday Life Through
     the Ages*. Pleasantville, NY: Reader's Digest
     Association Ltd., 1992.

Eason, Cassandra. *Candle Power*. London, England:
     Orion Publishing Group, 1999.

Farrar, Jane and Stewart. *Spells and How They Work*.
     Phoenix, Washington 1990.

Freethy, Ron. *Book of Plant Uses, Names and Folklore*.
     Tanager Books, NY: 1985.

Gordon, Leslie. *Green Magic*. New York, NY: Viking
     Press, 1977.

Gordon, Stuart. *Encyclopedia of Myths and Legends*.
     London, England: Headline Book Publishing,
     1993.

Hall, Manley P. *Secret Teachings of All Ages*.
     Philosophical Research Society, CA 1977.

Hutchinson, Ruth. *Everyday's a Holiday*. Harper and
     Brothers, NY: 1961.

Ketch, Tina. *Candle Lighting Encyclopedia*. Tina Ketch,
     GA: 1991.

————. *Feng Shui Candle Lighting*. CA: 1999.

Kunz, George Frederick. *Curious Lore of
     Precious Stones*. New York, NY: Dover
     Publications, 1971.

Leach, Maria, ed. *Standard Dictionary of Folklore, Mythology, and Legend.* New York, NY: Harper & Row, 1984.

Loewe, Michael and Carmen Blacker, eds. *Oracles and Divination.* Boulder CO: Shambhala, 1981.

Miller, Gastavus Hindman. *Ten Thousand Dreams Interpreted.* Chicago, IL: M.A. Donohuse & Co., 1931.

Mitford, Miranda Bruce. *Illustrated Book of Signs & Symbols.* New York, NY: DK Publishing, 1996.

Opie, Iona & Tatem, Moira. *A Dictionary of Superstitions.* New York, NY: Oxford University Press, 1989.

Oppenheimer, Betty. *The Candlemaker's Companion.* Storey Books, 1997.

Telesco, Patricia. *Futuretelling.* Freedom, CA: Crossing Press, 1997.

———. *Herbal Arts.* Secaucus, NJ: Citadel Books, 1997.

———. *Kitchen Witch's Cookbook.* St. Paul, MN: Llewellyn Publications, 1994.

———. *Spinning Spells: Weaving Wonders.* Freedom, CA: Crossing Press, 1996.

Walker, Barbara. *The Woman's Dictionary of Symbols & Sacred Objects.* SanFrancico CA: Harper & Row, 1988.

Waring, Philippa. *The Dictionary of Omens & Superstitions.* Secaucus, NJ: Chartwell Books, 1978.

Index

About the Author

Trish Telesco is the mother of three, wife, chief human to five pets, and a full-time professional author with numerous books on the market. These include the best selling *Exploring Candle Magick, Money Magick, An Enchanted Life, Gardening with the Goddess, A Witch's Beverages and Brews* and other diverse titles, each of which represents a different area of spiritual interest for her and her readers.

Trish considers herself a down-to-earth Kitchen Witch whose love of folklore and world-wide customs flavor every one of her spells and rituals. While her Wiccan education was originally self-trained and self-initiated, she later received initiation into the Strega tradition of Italy, which gives form and fullness to the folk magick Trish practices. Her strongest beliefs lie in following personal vision, being tolerant of other traditions, making life an act of worship, and being creative so that magick grows with you.

Trish travels at least twice a month to give lectures and workshops around the country. She has appeared and been featured on several television segments including

Sightings on muli-cultural divination systems, and *National Geographic Today–Solstice Celebrations*. All the while, Trish maintains a strong, visible presence in metaphysical journals including Circle Network News, and on the internet through popular sites such as *www.witchvox.com* (festival focus), her interactive home page *www.loresinger.com,* and yahoo club *www.groups.yahoo.com/groups/folkmagicwithtrishtelesco,* and various appearances on Internet chats and bbs boards.

Her hobbies include gardening, herbalism, brewing, singing, hand crafts, antique restoration, and landscaping. Her current project is helping support various Neo-Pagan causes, including land funds for religious retreats.